FOOD EDITORS' TREASURED

A Cookbook to Benefit the Better Homes™ Foundation

Library of Congress Catalog Card Number: 91-50610
ISBN: 0-696-02458-6

CONTRIBUTORS

These recipes are personal favorites of Meredith Corporation food editors and test kitchen home economists who work for the following publications:

BETTER HOMES AND GARDENS magazine:

Nancy Byal   Julia Malloy

Kristi Fuller   Joy Taylor

Lisa Holderness-Brown

BETTER HOMES AND GARDENS books:

Sandra Granseth   Heidi McNutt

Sharyl Heiken   Joyce Trollope

Rosemary Hutchinson   Liz Woolever

Shelli McConnell

BETTER HOMES AND GARDENS TEST KITCHEN:

Patty Beebout   Maryellyn Krantz

Lynn Blanchard   Mara Murphy

Kay Cargill   Jennifer Peterson

Judy Comstock   Sharon Stilwell

Marilyn Cornelius   Colleen Weeden

Janet Herwig

COUNTRY AMERICA magazine: Diane Yanney

COUNTRY HOME magazine: Lisa Kingsley

LADIES' HOME JOURNAL magazine:

Lisa Brainerd   Carol Prager

Jan Hazard   Susan Sarao–Westmoreland

MEREDITH PUBLISHING SERVICES: Lois White

MIDWEST LIVING magazine: Diana McMillen

METROPOLITAN HOME magazine: Christopher Hirsheimer

TRADITIONAL HOME magazine: Janet Figg

This book is possible thanks to the generous contributions of so many people. We especially want to thank **Meredith Corporation** for its financial support and for making this project to benefit homeless families a reality. In addition, we'd like to extend our gratitude to the following contributors:

BCI Book Covers, Chicago, Illinois: book cover board

Cedar Graphics, Cedar Rapids, Iowa: dust jacket printing

Champion International, Chicago, Illinois: end sheets, dust jacket paper

Dahl's Food Marts, Des Moines, Iowa: groceries for photography

Feiereisen, Inc., Cedar Rapids, Iowa: U.V. coating for dust jacket

Florist Supply Inc., Des Moines, Iowa: flowers for photography

Lake Book Manufacturing, Inc., Melrose Park, Illinois: book binding

Mid-City Litho, Lake Forest, Illinois: book cover printing

Orent Graphics, Omaha, Nebraska: four–color separations

Primary Image, Des Moines, Iowa: film and processing of photographs

R.R. Donnelley Printing Company L.P., Des Moines, Iowa: stripping and prepress work

Steenson & Associates, Des Moines, Iowa: nutritional analysis of recipes

Sun World International, Indio, California: produce for photography

FOOD EDITORS' TREASURED RECIPES

Editors: Nancy Byal, Kristi Fuller, Sharyl Heiken, Lisa Holderness-Brown, Julia Malloy, Shelli McConnell, Joy Taylor

Designers: Nancy Kluender, Mickie Vorhes

Illustrator: Nancy Kluender

Copy editor: David Walsh

Food stylist: Janet Herwig

Photographer: Scott Little

Production adviser: Jim Kalhorn

Production coordinator: Ivan McDonald

Editorial assistants: Rose Galbreath, Karen Pollock

On the cover: Custard Rum Torta (see recipe, page 112)

DEDICATION

This book is dedicated to David Jordan, Editor-in-Chief of Better Homes and Gardens® magazine and Chairman of the Board of the Better Homes™ Foundation, and Ellen L. Bassuk, M.D., President of the foundation. The book also is dedicated to all the resolute professionals and volunteers who work, day after day, to help homeless families return to mainstream community life.

PREFACE

Most of us haven't an inkling what it feels like to be without a home. But the growing problem of homelessness troubles us as we see its destructive effects on families in the cities, towns, and rural communities where we live. Even our pets are better fed, sheltered, and cared for than hundreds of thousands of children in this country who have no place to call home.

Since 1988, when the Better Homes™ Foundation was founded, BH&G® magazine readers have generously given their dollars, time, and talent to help solve this tragic national problem. School children raffled cookies and cakes they made; others collected and recycled cans. A quilt club handcrafted a special quilt and put it up for auction. BH&G real estate firms nationwide organized fund-raising yard sales.

This cookbook is one more step (and we hope a big one) toward funding the essential programs and services homeless families need to get back into mainstream American life. Food editors and test kitchen home economists throughout the Meredith Corporation family of publications—**Better Homes and Gardens** magazine, special interest publications, and books; **Country America; Country Home; Ladies' Home Journal;** Meredith Publishing Services; **Metropolitan Home; Midwest Living;** and **Traditional Home**—contributed recipes, a first-time-ever collaboration for us. The recipes, pulled from our personal files, represent the foods we love to cook and serve at home to our families and friends.

ADDITIONAL BOOK ORDERS

Proceeds from this book will help fund the Better Homes™ Foundation programs and services for homeless families all around the country. These include: preschool programs, such as infant and day care; medical, dental, vision, and hearing services for children; recreation and tutoring programs; job training, counseling, and parental workshops for parents; and programs that help adults find jobs and permanent housing for their families. The Better Homes™ Foundation also supports long-term transitional housing programs where families can live until back on their feet.

Please tell your friends and family about our cookbook so they, too, can contribute to the efforts of the Better Homes™ Foundation. To order additional copies of *FOOD EDITORS' TREASURED RECIPES*, send check or money order payable to The Better Homes™ Foundation for $14.95 plus $3.00 for postage and handling (Massachusetts and Iowa residents add state tax) to:

FOOD EDITORS' TREASURED RECIPES
P.O. Box 9236
Des Moines, IA 50306

CONTENTS

Wonderful Cheese and Apples (page 10) combines America's favorite fruit with three cheeses, sour cream, and walnuts.

APPETIZERS AND SNACKS

Entertaining these days can mean more than sitting down to a four-course dinner and dessert. Time spent with friends and family can be made special with fare as simple as a glass of wine and a delectable appetizer. Or, for drop-in guests, serve an impromptu snack. Whatever occasion arises, you'll find an appetizer or snack in this chapter to fit your style of entertaining.

WONDERFUL CHEESE AND APPLES

Since my family tends a 35-acre apple orchard, I'm always collecting apple recipes. The original version of this spread came from a California caterer who used Swiss and blue cheeses. You can make it ahead and freeze it for several months.

—Nancy Byal

Serves 16

   4 **ounces Camembert cheese (including rind), cut up**
   4 **ounces Gouda cheese, shredded (1 cup)**
   3 **8-ounce packages cream cheese**
   2 **tablespoons milk**
   2 **tablespoons dairy sour cream**
1¼ **cups chopped walnuts**
Snipped parsley
   6 **to 8 green *and/or* red apples**
Ascorbic acid color keeper *or* lemon juice mixed with water
Seedless green grapes (optional)

Let the cheeses stand at room temperature for 30 minutes. In a large mixing bowl combine Camembert, Gouda, and *2 packages* of the cream cheese; beat with an electric mixer on medium speed till mixed. Set aside.

Line a 9-inch flan pan, pie plate, cake pan, or quiche dish with foil or plastic wrap. Stir milk and sour cream into the remaining cream cheese; spread the mixture into the prepared pan. Sprinkle nuts atop; press nuts gently into mixture. Spoon Camembert mixture atop nuts, spreading to the edges of the pan. Place plastic wrap directly over cheese; seal tightly. Refrigerate overnight or up to three days before serving.

To serve, remove plastic wrap from top of cheese. Turn out onto a serving plate; remove foil or plastic wrap. Sprinkle with parsley. Slice apples into bite-size wedges; dip into color keeper or lemon juice mixed with water. Arrange apple slices and, if desired, grapes around cheese.

Per serving: *290 cal., 25 g fat (13 g sat. fat), 60 mg chol., 8 g pro., 11 g carbo., 2 g dietary fiber, 246 mg sodium.*

SOUTH-OF-THE-BORDER DIP

Serves 10 to 12

⅔ cup mayonnaise *or* salad dressing
¼ cup dairy sour cream
1 1¼-ounce package taco seasoning mix
1 9-ounce can jalapeño-flavored bean dip
1 8-ounce container sour cream dip with avocado
4 ounces shredded sharp cheddar cheese (1 cup)
4 ounces shredded Monterey Jack cheese (1 cup)
4 green onions, sliced
1 2¼-ounce can sliced pitted ripe olives, drained
Tortilla chips

In a small mixing bowl stir together mayonnaise or salad dressing, sour cream, and taco seasoning mix; set aside.

Spread the bean dip in the bottom of a 10-inch quiche dish or pie plate. Spread the sour cream dip with avocado over the bean layer; spread the mayonnaise mixture over the sour cream layer. Sprinkle with shredded cheddar cheese, shredded Monterey Jack cheese, the green onions, and olives. Cover and chill for up to 24 hours. Serve with tortilla chips.

Per serving: *418 cal., 32 g fat (11 g sat. fat), 43 mg chol., 11 g pro., 24 g carbo., 4 g dietary fiber, 620 mg sodium.*

Of all the Mexican-style dip recipes around, this personal top choice always gets many requests, even when served to fellow food editors. If you like it really hot, use Monterey Jack cheese with jalapeño peppers and add a few dashes of bottled hot pepper sauce. But you'd better have a margarita close by!

—Shelli McConnell

BEEFY SPINACH DIP

Serves 10 to 12

> 1 cup mayonnaise *or* salad dressing
> 1 cup dairy sour cream
> 1 3-ounce package cream cheese, softened
> 2 teaspoons dried dillweed
> 1½ teaspoons Beau Monde seasoning*
> 1 10-ounce package frozen chopped spinach, thawed and well drained
> ½ cup sliced green onions
> 1 2½-ounce package very thinly sliced dried beef, finely chopped
> 1 pound unsliced round loaf rye *or* sourdough bread
> Raw vegetable dippers *and/or* snack chips

For dip, in a large mixing bowl stir together mayonnaise or salad dressing, sour cream, cream cheese, dillweed, and Beau Monde seasoning. Stir in spinach, green onions, and dried beef. Cover and chill at least 4 hours or till serving time.

For bread bowl, slice 1 inch off top of bread. Hollow out center, leaving 1-inch thickness for sides and bottom, reserving center bread. Cut or tear reserved bread into bite-size pieces. To serve, spoon dip into the bread bowl. Serve with bread and fresh vegetables and/or snack chips.

Per serving: *375 cal., 27 g fat (8 g sat. fat), 46 mg chol., 9 g pro., 26 g carbo., 4 g dietary fiber, 857 mg sodium.*

*Note: *If you like, you can substitute ¾ teaspoon onion powder and ¾ teaspoon celery salt for the Beau Monde seasoning.*

CRAB-CHEESE DIP

Serves 14

    1 **8-ounce package cream cheese, softened**
    1 **6-ounce can crabmeat, drained, flaked, and cartilage removed**
    2 **tablespoons milk**
    2 **tablespoons dry sherry**
  ½ **teaspoon prepared mustard**
    2 **tablespoons snipped parsley**
Assorted vegetable dippers

In a small mixing bowl stir together cream cheese, crabmeat, milk, sherry, and mustard. Transfer to a serving bowl; sprinkle with parsley. Cover and chill for up to 24 hours or till serving time. (The dip may be frozen for up to 1 month.) Serve with assorted vegetables.

Per serving: *88 cal., 6 g fat (4 g sat. fat), 29 mg chol., 4 g pro., 4 g carbo., 1 g dietary fiber, 105 mg sodium.*

This dip is a lifesaver for an impromptu dinner party. Just take the dip out of the freezer, thaw it for several hours in the refrigerator, and sprinkle it with parsley on its way to the table.

—Rosemary Hutchinson

BOBOLI WITH ONIONS AND BLUE CHEESE

Serves 12

    1 **large onion, thinly sliced and separated into rings**
    2 **tablespoons margarine *or* butter**
    1 **teaspoon sugar**
    3 **6-inch Boboli shells**
    1 **tablespoon olive oil**
  ¼ **to ½ cup crumbled blue cheese**
    1 **teaspoon dried rosemary, crushed**

In a small skillet cook onion rings in margarine or butter till almost tender. Add sugar; cook about 5 minutes more or till onions are golden and very tender. Remove from heat.

Brush the Boboli shells with a little olive oil. Spread onion mixture on each shell; top with blue cheese and rosemary. Transfer to a baking sheet. Bake in a 400° oven about 10 minutes or till hot. To serve, cut into wedges.

Per serving: *116 cal., 5 g fat (1 g sat. fat), 3 mg chol., 4 g pro., 14 g carbo., 1 g dietary fiber, 211 mg sodium.*

This quick appetizer scores big when we gather to cheer on our favorite Super Bowl team. Look for the ready-to-use Boboli shells in the refrigerated case or bread section of your supermarket. If small shells are unavailable, use one large shell.

—Joy Taylor

SPINACH-AND-HAM APPETIZER PIE

Serves 16

    1 15-ounce package folded refrigerated unbaked piecrusts (2 crusts)
    1 12-ounce package frozen spinach soufflé
    1 cup finely chopped fully cooked ham
    ½ of an 8-ounce can sliced water chestnuts, drained and finely chopped
Milk

Let piecrusts stand at room temperature for 10 to 15 minutes. Meanwhile, remove soufflé from foil tray; place in a 1-quart microwave-safe casserole. Micro-cook on 30% power (medium-low) for 5 minutes. Use a fork to break up soufflé. Cook for 3 to 5 minutes more or till soufflé is thawed, stirring once.

Unfold piecrusts and remove paper; place one crust on an ungreased baking sheet. Spread soufflé mixture over crust, leaving a 1-inch border. Sprinkle with ham and water chestnuts. Moisten edges of crust with water.

Using an hors d'oeuvre cutter, cut decorative shapes from second crust, reserving cutouts. Place cut-out crust atop filling. Seal edges with tines of a fork. Place reserved cutouts atop pie. Brush top with milk. Bake in a 375° oven for 25 to 30 minutes or till golden. Cool slightly. Cut into wedges; serve warm.

Per serving: *171 cal., 11 g fat (9 g sat. fat), 34 mg chol., 5 g pro., 13 g carbo., 1 g dietary fiber, 341 mg sodium.*

SHRIMP ROLLS

Makes 40 to 50

  1 **8-ounce package cream cheese, softened**
  1 **4½-ounce can shrimp, rinsed, drained, and finely chopped,** *or* **4 ounces**
      cooked and shelled shrimp, finely chopped
 ¼ **cup shredded Swiss** *or* **Gouda cheese**
 ¼ **cup seeded and finely chopped cucumber**
  2 **tablespoons sliced green onion**
  4 **to 6 medium flour tortillas**
Cocktail sauce

In a medium mixing bowl stir together the cream cheese, finely chopped shrimp, shredded Swiss or Gouda cheese, chopped cucumber, and sliced green onion. Spread about ¼ *cup* of the shrimp mixture onto *each* flour tortilla. Roll up each tortilla jelly-roll style. Place filled tortillas, seam side down, in a shallow pan. Cover with plastic wrap and chill for several hours or overnight.

To serve, slice tortillas into ½-inch-thick slices. Serve with cocktail sauce.

Per serving: *35 cal., 2 g fat (1 g sat. fat), 14 mg chol., 2 g pro., 2 g carbo., 0 g dietary fiber, 37 mg sodium.*

Party suggestion: *For a make-ahead appetizer spread, fix this easy recipe in addition to Zippy Party Nuts (page 19) and Wonderful Cheese and Apples (page 10). Boboli with Onions and Blue Cheese (page 13) also would go well with these recipes, but can't be fixed ahead.*

With this make-ahead snack, there is little last-minute preparation before party guests arrive. Arrange the mini-pinwheels on a lettuce-lined serving platter. Then, set out a bowl of cocktail sauce so everyone can dab a bit onto each roll.

—Diane Yanney

MARINATED COCKTAIL SHRIMP

Serves 6

- 1 pound fresh *or* frozen large shrimp in shells
- ¼ cup snipped fresh cilantro
- ¼ cup olive oil *or* salad oil
- 3 tablespoons wine vinegar
- 2 tablespoons lemon juice
- 1 fresh jalapeño pepper, seeded and finely chopped, *or* 1 tablespoon chopped canned jalapeño pepper
- 2 teaspoons capers, drained
- 1 clove garlic, minced
- 1 small lemon, halved lengthwise and sliced
- 1 small lime, halved lengthwise and sliced
- 1 small red onion, halved and thinly sliced

In a large saucepan cook fresh or frozen shrimp, uncovered, in lightly salted boiling water for 1 to 3 minutes or till shrimp turn pink. Drain and cool. Peel shrimp, leaving tails intact; devein and set aside.

For marinade, in a screw-top jar combine cilantro, oil, vinegar, lemon juice, jalapeño pepper, capers, and garlic. Cover and shake well to mix. Set aside.

To serve, in a large serving bowl layer sliced lemon, lime, red onion, and the shrimp, repeating till all is used. Drizzle marinade atop. Cover and chill for at least 4 hours or overnight.

Per serving: *166 cal., 10 g fat (1 g sat. fat), 148 mg chol., 17 g pro., 3 g carbo., 0 g dietary fiber, 205 mg sodium.*

For a romantic picnic or special get-together, serve this beautiful appetizer with champagne, crusty French bread, and assorted cheeses. Or, you can serve it as a refreshing summer meal.

—Lisa Holderness-Brown

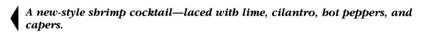

A new-style shrimp cocktail—laced with lime, cilantro, hot peppers, and capers.

GRILLED TUNA WITH WHITE BEANS

Where iceburg lettuce and frozen fish once ruled, arugula and fresh tuna now are staples. At a recent *Metropolitan Home* party, guests couldn't line up fast enough for a bite of these open-face sandwiches. If you like the idea, make it your own by adding different greens.

—*Christopher Hirsheimer*

Serves 16 to 24

½ **pound fresh tuna steak**
Olive oil
Freshly ground black pepper
 1 **15-ounce can cannellini beans, drained**
Peel of 1 lemon, finely shredded
Dash salt
Dash pepper
Juice of 1 lemon
 ¼ **cup fresh flat-leaf parsley (Italian parsley), chopped**
 1 **bunch arugula, trimmed, washed, and patted dry**
16 to 24 **small slices French bread**
Fresh flat-leaf parsley (Italian parsley)

Rub tuna steak with a little olive oil. Generously sprinkle both sides of fish with pepper; press onto fish. Grill fish directly over *hot* coals till fish flakes when tested with a fork. (*Or,* cook fish in a small skillet over high heat till it flakes when tested with a fork.) Allow 6 to 9 minutes for each ½ inch of thickness.

Meanwhile, in a small mixing bowl combine the drained beans, *2 tablespoons* of olive oil, *½ teaspoon* lemon peel, salt, and pepper.

Place the grilled tuna in a small bowl; drizzle with a little olive oil and with lemon juice. Sprinkle with parsley and remaining lemon peel.

To serve, brush the bread with a little olive oil; toast under broiler or on grill till golden brown. Remove tuna from lemon mixture, reserving mixture; cut tuna into 16 to 24 slices. Top each bread slice with arugula, beans, and a slice of tuna. Drizzle with reserved lemon juice mixture. Garnish with additional parsley.

Per serving: *257 cal., 10 g fat (2 g sat. fat), 11 mg chol., 13 g pro., 29 g carbo., 4 g dietary fiber, 217 mg sodium.*

ZIPPY PARTY NUTS

Serves 8

　1 tablespoon margarine *or* butter, melted
　1 teaspoon salt
　1 teaspoon Worcestershire sauce
　⅛ teaspoon ground red pepper
Several dashes bottled hot pepper sauce
　2 cups nuts (walnut halves, raw peanuts, raw cashews,
　　　pumpkin seeds, pecan halves, *and/or* blanched whole almonds)

In a large bowl combine melted margarine with salt, Worcestershire sauce, red pepper, and hot pepper sauce. Add nuts; stir till coated. Spread nuts on a large baking sheet. Bake in a 325° oven for 15 minutes, stirring twice. Remove from oven. Using a spatula, toss the nuts. Cool.

Per serving: *206 cal., 20 g fat (2 g sat. fat), 0 mg chol., 4 g pro., 6 g carbo., 1 g dietary fiber, 293 mg sodium.*

These zesty mixed nuts always are a welcomed nibble at parties. They're great just for snacking, too. Make sure you have enough on hand because they disappear fast!

—Kristi Fuller

SPICED CHERRY CIDER

Serves 18

　8 cups cherry-flavored apple cider
　4 cups strong brewed tea
　½ of a 6-ounce can frozen orange juice concentrate
　½ of a 6-ounce can frozen lemonade concentrate
　½ cup sugar
　3 inches cinnamon stick
　1 teaspoon whole cloves

In a large kettle combine 8 cups *water* with the cider, tea, juice concentrates, and sugar. Place cinnamon and cloves in cheesecloth and tie; add to cider mixture. Bring mixture to boiling; reduce heat. Cover and simmer for 20 minutes.

Per serving: *91 cal., 0 g fat (0 g sat. fat), 0 mg chol., 0 g pro., 23 g carbo., 0 g dietary fiber, 5 mg sodium.*

Our family cheers the holidays with this hot toddy on cold, wintry nights. If cherry cider is unavailable, apple cider works great, too.

—Lynn Blanchard

Grilled Salmon Steaks with Summer Salsa (page 22)—a tasty choice for outdoor dining with friends.

ENTRÉES FOR ENTERTAINING

Putting on a special meal for friends and family is a popular activity for many food editors. It gives each of us a chance to show off one of our latest edible innovations. But, like many cooks, we often don't have much discretionary time. That's why, along with the go-all-out entrées in the chapter, you'll also find timesaving techniques and make-ahead guests-are-coming recipes. From elegant chicken dishes to delightful brunch ideas, we wish you sparkling company meals with this special recipe collection.

GRILLED SALMON STEAKS WITH SUMMER SALSA

After we spent three days of Alaskan fishing several years ago, our home freezer was stocked with 40 pounds of salmon steaks and fillets. That summer, grilled fish was a recurring menu item at our house, and we never tired of it, especially with a tasty marinade and salsa to go with it.

—Joy Taylor

Serves 4

4 fresh *or* frozen salmon steaks, cut ¾ inch thick (about 1½ pounds)
1 recipe Summer Salsa (below)
2 oranges
⅔ cup dry white wine
¼ cup avocado oil *or* olive oil
2 teaspoons minced dried onion
2 teaspoons snipped fresh rosemary *or* ½ teaspoon dried rosemary, crushed
Grilled new potatoes (optional)
Fresh rosemary sprigs (optional)

Thaw fish, if frozen. Prepare Summer Salsa; cover and chill till serving time. For marinade, finely shred enough peel from one orange to make *1 teaspoon*. Juice the oranges. In a shallow dish stir together the 1 teaspoon orange peel, the juice, wine, oil, onion, rosemary, and ¼ teaspoon *each* of *salt* and *pepper*. Add salmon; turn once to coat. Cover and refrigerate about 1 hour, turning fish steaks once or twice.

To grill: Remove fish from marinade. Grill fish on an uncovered grill directly over *medium-hot* coals for 6 to 9 minutes or till fish flakes easily when tested with a fork, turning fish once and brushing with marinade during grilling. Serve fish with salsa and grilled potatoes. Garnish with fresh rosemary.

Per serving: *584 cal., 41 g fat (6 g sat. fat), 99 mg chol., 33 g pro., 17 g carbo., 7 g dietary fiber, 149 mg sodium.*

SUMMER SALSA

Makes 1 cup

2 oranges
1 medium avocado, peeled, seeded, and cubed
1 medium tomato, chopped
2 tablespoons avocado oil *or* olive oil
1 teaspoon snipped fresh rosemary *or* pinch dried rosemary
Dash pepper

Peel oranges. Working over a small bowl, section oranges, catching juices in bowl. Add the remaining ingredients; toss gently. Cover and chill.

FISH STEAKS DIJON

Serves 4

- **4 fresh *or* frozen halibut, salmon, *or* swordfish steaks, cut ¾ inch thick (about 1½ pounds)**
- **¼ cup dry white wine**
- **3 tablespoons cooking oil**
- **3 tablespoons lemon juice**
- **2 tablespoons country-style Dijon mustard**
- **2 tablespoons sliced green onion**
- **¼ teaspoon pepper**

Lemon wedges

Thaw fish, if frozen. In a shallow dish combine the white wine, cooking oil, lemon juice, mustard, green onion, and pepper. Place fish steaks in the marinade. Turn fish to coat with marinade. Cover and chill fish in the refrigerator at least 2 hours or overnight, turning fish once. At serving time, drain fish steaks, reserving the marinade. Cook as desired and serve with lemon wedges.

To grill: Cook steaks on an uncovered grill directly over *medium-hot* coals for 6 to 9 minutes or till fish flakes easily with a fork, turning fish once and brushing with reserved marinade during grilling.

To broil: Preheat broiler. Place fish on the greased unheated rack of a broiler pan. Brush with reserved marinade. Broil 4 inches from heat for 6 to 9 minutes or till fish flakes easily when tested with a fork, turning fish once and brushing with reserved marinade during broiling.

Per serving: *295 cal., 16 g fat (2 g sat. fat), 52 mg chol., 36 g pro., 4 g carbo., 0 g dietary fiber, 322 mg sodium.*

Note: *For fish kabobs, thread fish cubes on 4 long or 8 medium skewers with desired vegetables, leaving about ¼ inch between pieces. For vegetables, try cubed sweet pepper, pea pods, and/or precooked baby carrots, potato wedges, or zucchini slices. Allow 8 to 10 minutes total cooking time for the kabobs.*

We often turn to this recipe for entertaining because it's so adaptable. We can cook the fish on the grill outdoors or under the broiler indoors, depending on the weather. Sometimes we buy two or three kinds of fish steaks, and cut them into cubes before marinating. That way, we serve mixed fish kabobs.

—Janet Herwig

CHICKEN WITH CAPER CREAM

When I'm cooking for friends, this recipe is my old faithful. It's so quick to fix—just 20 minutes of prep time and 25 minutes cooking time— and I always know that my guests will love it.

—Jan Hazard

Serves 4

> 2 tablespoons margarine *or* butter
> 4 chicken breast halves
> 2 tablespoons white wine vinegar
> ¾ cup whipping cream
> 1 tablespoon capers, drained
> ½ bay leaf
> ½ teaspoon dried oregano, crushed
> ¼ teaspoon freshly ground pepper
> Oregano and parsley sprigs (optional)

In a large skillet melt margarine or butter over medium heat. Add chicken and cook until brown, about 4 minutes per side. Transfer to a shallow baking dish; set aside. Pour off drippings from skillet. Add vinegar to skillet and cook for 30 seconds. Stir in cream, capers, bay leaf, oregano, and pepper. Heat to boiling, stirring to loosen browned bits from bottom of skillet; boil for 2 minutes. Pour caper cream sauce over chicken. Bake, uncovered, in a 350° oven about 25 minutes or till chicken is no longer pink. Discard bay leaf. Garnish each serving with a sprig of fresh herb, if desired.

Per serving: *322 cal., 25 g fat (15 g sat. fat), 130 mg chol., 21 g pro., 3 g carbo., 0 g dietary fiber, 144 mg sodium.*

Menu suggestion: *Serve lightly dressed side dishes with this rich entrée. For instance, in the springtime, prepare steamed asparagus spears and basmati rice to accompany the chicken. In winter, steamed brussels sprouts and wild rice pilaf would be a good choice. A fresh-fruit dessert wins any time of the year.*

PECAN PARMESAN CHICKEN

Serves 8

Nonstick spray coating
8 medium boneless, skinless chicken breast halves (1½ pounds total)
⅔ cup grated Parmesan cheese
½ cup finely chopped pecans *or* walnuts
¼ cup fine dry Italian-seasoned bread crumbs
1 teaspoon dried thyme, basil, *or* marjoram, crushed (optional)
2 slightly beaten egg whites
2 tablespoons water

Spray a 13x9x2-inch baking dish with nonstick coating; set aside. Rinse chicken; pat dry. In a small bowl combine Parmesan cheese, pecans or walnuts, and bread crumbs; add herb, if desired. In another small bowl combine egg whites and water. Dip chicken breast halves into the egg mixture, then coat with Parmesan mixture. Arrange chicken in the prepared baking dish. Sprinkle any remaining Parmesan mixture over the chicken. (Cover and refrigerate chicken at this point, if desired, for up to 12 hours.) Bake, uncovered, in a 350° oven about 40 minutes or till chicken is tender and no longer pink. Use a spatula to transfer chicken to dinner plates.

Per serving: *204 cal., 10 g fat (3 g sat. fat), 59 mg chol., 24 g pro., 4 g carbo., 1 g dietary fiber, 197 mg sodium.*

Menu suggestion: *This Italian-seasoned main dish goes well with a variety of foods. A pasta side dish is a natural. Try spaghetti with a tomatoey sauce or a fun-shaped pasta, such as bow ties, with a cream sauce. For a vegetable accompaniment, serve steamed broccoli or zucchini dressed with olive oil and Parmesan cheese.*

I usually coat the chicken pieces several hours ahead, and chill them in the baking dish. When company arrives there is no messy, last-minute hassle. The chicken bakes without any attention. leaving plenty of time to entertain. Plus, my boys love Parmesan, so they'll eat this dish when friends come for dinner.

—Liz Woolever

STUFFED CHICKEN WITH GINGER CREAM

Serves 8

    4 whole medium chicken breasts
    8 ounces boneless, skinless chicken thighs
    2 eggs
    2 cups whipping cream
    ¼ teaspoon salt
    ⅛ teaspoon pepper
    1 tablespoon chopped shallots
    1 tablespoon margarine *or* butter
    1 cup dry white wine
    1 slice fresh gingerroot, about ¼ inch thick
    2 cups chicken broth
    2 medium leeks, thinly sliced
    1 tablespoon lemon juice
    ¼ cup margarine *or* butter
    1 recipe Light and Lemony Fettuccine (see page 84)

Bone the chicken breasts, leaving skin intact. In a food processor grind chicken thighs. With processor running, add eggs, *1 cup* of the cream, the salt, and pepper. Process till well blended. Stuff thigh mixture between skin and meat of each breast. Cover and refrigerate for 1 to 4 hours.

At serving time, in a 12-inch skillet cook shallots in the 1 tablespoon margarine or butter till tender. Stir in wine and gingerroot. Bring to boiling; reduce heat. Boil for 4 to 5 minutes or till reduced by half (you should have about ½ cup). Add broth to skillet. Bring to boiling. Using a large spatula, lower stuffed breasts carefully into broth mixture. Reduce heat. Cover; simmer for 40 minutes. Remove chicken; keep warm. Add leeks to broth in skillet; boil to reduce to about 1½ cups. Remove gingerroot. Add remaining 1 cup whipping cream to skillet. Boil to reduce by ⅓ (should have about 1¾ cups). Stir in lemon juice. Remove from heat. Add remaining butter, 1 tablespoon at a time, stirring after each addition till butter is melted and mixture is thickened.

To serve, cut each breast in half lengthwise. Place each portion atop Light and Lemony Fettuccine. Spoon sauce over all.

Per serving: *599 cal., 40 g fat (21 g sat. fat), 239 mg chol., 29 g pro., 28 g carbo., 2 g dietary fiber, 440 mg sodium.*

WARM CHICKEN AND ARUGULA SALAD

Serves 4

⅓ cup balsamic vinegar *or* red wine vinegar
¼ cup olive oil *or* salad oil
2 teaspoons sugar
1 teaspoon coarse-grain brown mustard *or* Dijon-style mustard
⅛ teaspoon black pepper
1 to 2 tablespoons olive oil *or* salad oil
2 skinless, boneless chicken breast halves, cut into bite-size strips
1 clove garlic, minced
1 teaspoon lemon juice (optional)
½ teaspoon herb-pepper seasoning
7 to 8 cups torn assorted greens
1 cup torn arugula
1 medium red, yellow, *or* orange sweet pepper, cut into thin, 2-inch strips
Homemade Croutons

For dressing, in a screw-top jar combine vinegar, the ¼ cup oil, the sugar, mustard, and black pepper. Cover; shake well. In a skillet heat the 1 to 2 tablespoons oil over medium heat. Add chicken, garlic, lemon juice, and herb-pepper seasonings. Stir-fry about 3 minutes or till chicken is no longer pink. Divide greens and arugula among four dinner plates. Top with chicken, pepper strips, and croutons. Pass the dressing.

Per serving: *474 cal., 33 g fat (6 g sat. fat), 38 mg chol., 20 g pro., 25 g carbo., 3 g dietary fiber, 450 mg sodium.*

HOMEMADE CROUTONS

Makes 2 cups

¼ cup margarine *or* butter
2 tablespoons grated Parmesan cheese
⅛ teaspoon garlic powder
4 ½-inch slices French bread, cut into ¾-inch cubes

In a large skillet melt margarine or butter. Remove from heat. Stir in Parmesan cheese and garlic powder. Add bread cubes; stir till coated. Spread bread cubes in a shallow baking pan. Bake in a 300° oven for 10 minutes. Stir. Bake 5 minutes more or till crisp. Store croutons in an airtight container for up to 1 week.

This salad, along with crusty sourdough bread and a glass of chardonnay wine, is my best toss-together dinner for weeknight meals with friends. For the mixed greens, you can use any salad green you have on hand. I often use spinach, romaine, or green leaf lettuce.

—Lisa Holderness-Brown

HOT CHICKEN SALAD WITH JALAPEÑO DRESSING

Serves 4

- ½ cup mayonnaise *or* salad dressing
- 2 tablespoons honey
- 1 tablespoon lemon juice
- ½ to 1 teaspoon finely chopped and seeded fresh *or* canned jalapeño pepper
- ¼ teaspoon dry mustard
- ¼ teaspoon paprika
- 4 large boneless, skinless chicken breast halves

Lemon-pepper seasoning
- 1 tablespoon cooking oil
- 1 avocado

Lemon juice

Flowering kale leaves
- 8 to 12 strawberries, halved
- 2 apricots *or* peaches, cut into wedges
- 2 kiwi fruit, peeled and sliced
- 1 star fruit (carambola), sliced

For dressing, in a blender container or food processor bowl combine the the mayonnaise or salad dressing, honey, 1 tablespoon lemon juice, the jalapeño pepper, mustard, and paprika; cover and blend or process till smooth. Transfer to a small bowl or pitcher. Chill.

Sprinkle both sides of the chicken breasts lightly with lemon-pepper seasoning. In a large skillet cook chicken in hot oil over medium-high heat about 6 minutes per side or till golden brown and no longer pink in center.

To serve, seed, peel, and slice avocado; brush avocado slices with lemon juice. Line each dinner plate with kale leaves; place a warm chicken breast half on each plate. Arrange avocado, strawberries, apricots or peaches, kiwi fruit, and star fruit on each plate. Serve with jalapeño dressing.

Per serving: *552 cal., 38 g fat (6 g sat. fat), 88 mg chol., 29 g pro., 28 g carbo., 9 g dietary fiber, 243 mg sodium.*

Fresh and colorful ingredients help make a dish more appealing. So, go ahead and vary the fresh fruit and greens that accompany this chicken dish, according to the season and market availability.

—Janet Herwig

◀ **The spiced dressing and chilled fruits turn chicken into a provocative dinner.**

TURKEY AND SAUSAGE GUMBO

My teen years were spent in Louisiana, where friends introduced my family to Cajun cooking. Although the bayous are now far away, I still like to share a steaming pot of classic gumbo with friends. Serve it as the Cajuns do—in a bowl over rice, along with a crispy green salad.

—*Julia Malloy*

Serves 12

½ cup cooking oil
½ cup all-purpose flour
1 pound smoked sausage, cut into ½-inch slices and quartered
2 cups sliced okra *or* one 10-ounce package frozen cut okra, thawed
2 large green sweet peppers, chopped
2 large onions, chopped
1 cup chopped celery
4 cloves garlic, minced
3 bay leaves
2 teaspoons dried thyme, crushed
½ teaspoon salt
½ teaspoon ground black pepper
¼ teaspoon ground red pepper
6 cups water
2 16-ounce cans tomatoes, cut up
4 cups cubed cooked turkey *or* chicken
1 8-ounce package frozen, peeled, deveined shrimp
Hot cooked rice

For roux, in a small cast-iron or heavy-duty skillet, heat oil over medium-high heat till almost smoking. Stir in flour; cook and stir constantly about 5 minutes or till the mixture starts to brown. Reduce heat to medium. Cook and stir about 15 minutes more or till a dark reddish-brown roux forms.

Meanwhile, in a 4-quart Dutch oven cook sausage till brown; drain on paper towels, reserving *1 tablespoon* drippings in pan. To drippings, add okra, sweet peppers, onions, celery, garlic, bay leaves, thyme, salt, black pepper, and red pepper; cook till onion is tender but not brown, stirring often. Stir in water, *undrained* tomatoes, and turkey or chicken; bring to boiling.

Slowly stir about *1 cup* of hot liquid into roux; stir roux into gumbo. Return to a gentle boil. Cover and simmer for 30 minutes. Add shrimp; cook about 5 minutes more or till shrimp turn pink. Season to taste with salt and pepper. Remove bay leaves. Serve in bowls over hot cooked rice.

Per serving without rice: *332 cal., 20 g fat (5 g sat. fat), 81 mg chol., 25 g pro., 13 g carbo., 2 g dietary fiber, 677 mg sodium.*

CASSOULET WITH DUCK AND LAMB

Serves 8 to 10

   1 **pound dry great northern beans (about 2⅓ cups)**
   1 **onion, studded with 2 cloves**
   1 **bay leaf**
   1 **teaspoon salt**
   1 **5- to 6-pound domestic duckling, cut up**
   1 **pound boneless lean pork, cubed**
   1 **pound boneless lean lamb, cubed**
   1 **cup chopped onion**
   ½ **cup chopped carrot**
   4 **teaspoons minced garlic, divided**
   1 **14½-ounce can chicken broth**
   1 **14½-ounce can tomatoes, cut up**
   1 **cup dry white wine**
   2 **teaspoons salt**
   1 **teaspoon freshly ground pepper**
   ½ **teaspoon dried thyme, crushed**
   ½ **cup dry bread crumbs**
   ¼ **cup snipped parsley**

Rinse beans. In a 4½-quart Dutch oven combine beans and enough *water* to cover. Bring to boiling; reduce heat. Simmer for 2 minutes. Remove from heat. Cover and let stand 1 hour. Drain and rinse beans.

In same Dutch oven combine soaked beans with 6 cups *fresh water.* Add onion with cloves and bay leaf. Simmer, uncovered, 30 minutes. Add the 1 teaspoon salt and simmer 30 minutes more. Drain beans; transfer to a bowl. Discard onion and bay leaf.

Meanwhile, in large Dutch oven brown the duck pieces, skin side down, over medium-high heat about 10 minutes. Remove duck from Dutch oven. Cook pork in drippings about 10 minutes or till brown. Remove pork. Brown lamb in drippings about 10 minutes. Remove lamb. Drain fat from Dutch oven. Add onion and carrot to Dutch oven. Cook over medium heat about 5 minutes or till tender. Add *3 teaspoons* of the garlic and cook for 30 seconds more. Return the duck, pork, and lamb to Dutch oven. Add chicken broth, *undrained* tomatoes, wine, the 2 teaspoons salt, pepper, and thyme. Bring to boiling; reduce heat. Cover and simmer for 1 hour.

Add beans to Dutch oven. Simmer, covered, 1 hour or till beans are tender.

To serve, in a small bowl combine bread crumbs, parsley, and remaining garlic. Preheat broiler. Transfer cassoulet to a shallow ovenproof serving dish. Top with crumb mixture and broil about 2 minutes or till brown.

Per serving: *777 cal., 38 g fat (13 g sat. fat), 159 mg chol., 60 g pro., 44 g carbo., 11 g dietary fiber, 1,157 mg sodium.*

Every year I can't wait for winter so I can make this simpler version of the French classic. It does take time (the perfect project for a cold weekend), but nothing beats its flavor. Allow 45 minutes of prep time and about 2½ hours of cooking.

—Lisa Brainerd

SPICY BEEF AND ASPARAGUS

When spring and asparagus season roll around, I treat my guests to this spicy stir-fry. For entertaining, we try different kinds of fresh or dried mushrooms—oyster, shiitake, porcini, tree ears, or straw mushrooms.

—Julia Malloy

Serves 4 to 6

1 pound boneless beef top round steak
1 tablespoon cornstarch
1 tablespoon dry sherry
1 tablespoon soy sauce
1 tablespoon hoisin sauce
1 teaspoon vinegar
½ teaspoon sugar
⅛ teaspoon ground red pepper
1 to 2 tablespoons cooking oil
3 cloves garlic, minced
2 teaspoons grated gingerroot *or* ¼ teaspoon ground ginger
12 ounces fresh asparagus, cut into 1-inch lengths (2 cups), *or* one 10-ounce package frozen cut asparagus, thawed
1 cup thinly sliced fresh shiitake mushrooms *or* one 15-ounce can straw mushrooms, drained
¼ cup thinly sliced green onion

Partially freeze beef; thinly slice across the grain into bite-size strips and set aside. In a 2-cup measure stir together cornstarch, sherry, soy sauce, hoisin sauce, vinegar, sugar, and red pepper; set aside.

Preheat a wok or large skillet over high heat; add 1 tablespoon oil. (Add more oil as necessary during cooking.) Stir-fry garlic and gingerroot in hot oil for 15 seconds. Add asparagus, mushrooms, and green onion; stir-fry for 4 to 6 minutes or till asparagus is crisp-tender. Remove vegetables; set aside.

Add *half* of the beef to hot wok or skillet; stir-fry for 2 to 3 minutes or till meat is brown. Remove meat. Stir-fry remaining beef for 2 to 3 minutes or till brown. Return all of the meat to wok or skillet; push meat from the center.

Stir soy sauce mixture; add to the center of the wok. Cook and stir till thickened and bubbly. Return vegetables to wok; stir to coat beef and vegetables with sauce. Cover and cook for 1 minute or just till heated through. Serve at once.

Per serving: *250 cal., 8 g fat (2 g sat. fat), 71 mg chol., 31 g pro., 14 g carbo., 2 g dietary fiber, 408 mg sodium.*

GRILLED LEMON FLANK STEAK

Serves 6

- 1 1- to 1½-pound beef flank steak
- 1 teaspoon finely shredded lemon peel
- ⅓ cup lemon juice
- ¼ cup sliced green onions
- 1 tablespoon sugar
- 1 tablespoon cooking oil
- 1 teaspoon coarse-grain brown *or* prepared mustard
- 1 teaspoon Worcestershire sauce
- ¼ teaspoon salt
- ¼ teaspoon pepper

Score meat by making shallow cuts at 1-inch intervals diagonally across the steak in a diamond pattern. Repeat scoring on opposite side. Place meat in a shallow bag set into a shallow dish.

For marinade, in a small mixing bowl combine lemon peel, lemon juice, green onions, sugar, cooking oil, mustard, Worcestershire sauce, salt, and pepper. Pour marinade over steak. Seal bag. Marinate at room temperature for 30 minutes or in the refrigerator for 6 to 24 hours, turning the bag occasionally.

Drain meat, reserving marinade. Grill steak on an uncovered grill directly over *medium* coals for 12 to 14 minutes or till medium-rare, turning once and brushing occasionally with the reserved marinade. (*Or,* broil the meat on the unheated rack of a broiler pan 4 to 5 inches from the heat for 12 to 14 minutes or till medium-rare, turning once and brushing occasionally with the reserved marinade.)

To serve, slice thinly across the grain.

Per serving: *152 cal., 8 g fat (3 g sat. fat), 38 mg chol., 16 g pro., 4 g carbo., 0 g dietary fiber, 156 mg sodium.*

Serving suggestion: *Arrange the thin slices of beef on a serving platter, then dress it up with green onion brushes and lemon slices. Let diners serve themselves for easy buffet entertaining.*

Come summer, this grilled dinner fits the way we entertain. Of course, I marinate it early in the day, leaving out last-minute work. And, while the steak grills, our company can sit outside on the deck and savor the aroma. The refreshing flavor always hits the spot.

—Liz Woolever

IOWA CHOPS WITH MAYTAG BLUE CHEESE SAUCE

As the food editor for the Des Moines-based **Midwest Living** *magazine, I must include an Iowa favorite. I always dish up steaming rutabaga and carrots alongside the chops and ladle some sauce over it all. Amazingly, my 5-year-old gobbles up the vegetables with gusto.*

—Diana McMillen

Serves 4

    4 pork loin chops, cut 1 to 1¼ inches thick
    2 medium carrots, cut into julienne strips
    1 small rutabaga (8 ounces), cut into julienne strips
    1 small tomato, peeled, seeded, and chopped
    ¼ teaspoon sugar
    1 clove garlic, minced
    2 tablespoons margarine *or* butter
    4 teaspoons all-purpose flour
    ¾ cup milk
    1 tablespoon snipped parsley
    ½ cup crumbled blue cheese (2 ounces)
  Fresh sage sprigs (optional)

Place chops on the rack of unheated broiler pan; broil chops 3 to 4 inches from heat for 14 minutes. Season with pepper. Turn meat; broil for 12 to 14 minutes more or till done. Meanwhile, cook carrots and rutabaga in a small amount of boiling salted water for 10 minutes.

For sauce, sprinkle tomato with sugar; set aside. In a small saucepan cook garlic in margarine or butter for 1 minute. Stir in flour. Add milk; cook and stir till thickened and bubbly. Cook and stir for 1 minute more. Stir in tomato and parsley. Heat through. Stir in *¼ cup* of the blue cheese. Serve sauce over chops. Sprinkle remaining cheese atop. Serve with carrots and rutabaga. Garnish with sage, if desired.

Per serving: *389 cal., 20 g fat (10 g sat. fat), 118 mg chol., 41 g pro., 14 g carbo., 3 g dietary fiber, 373 mg sodium.*

From the heartland with love. ▶

COUNTRY CHOPS AND PEPPERS

The casualness of this recipe reflects my preference for down-home entertaining on our farm. When friends stay for dinner, it tends to be impromptu. This dish is one I can whip up quickly.

—Nancy Byal

Serves 4

4 pork loin chops, cut ¾ inch thick (about 1½ pounds)
Salt-free lemon-pepper seasoning
Nonstick spray coating
1 medium red *or* green sweet pepper, cut into rings
¼ cup bias-sliced green onions
1 tablespoon margarine *or* butter
⅓ cup white wine Worcestershire sauce

Sprinkle pork chops lightly on both sides with lemon-pepper seasoning; press gently onto meat. Spray a large cold skillet with nonstick coating. Heat skillet. Cook chops in hot skillet over medium-high heat for 5 minutes. Turn chops. Top with red pepper and green onion. Cover and cook for 5 to 7 minutes more or till meat is no longer pink and vegetables are crisp-tender. Remove meat and vegetables; keep warm.

Melt margarine in hot skillet, scraping up crusty bits. Add Worcestershire sauce. Cook and stir over medium heat till mixture thickens slightly. Remove from heat.

To serve, place a pork chop on each dinner plate. Top with vegetables. Pour some sauce over each serving. Serve at once.

Per serving: *214 cal., 10 g fat (3 g sat. fat), 66 mg chol., 27 g pro., 7 g carbo., 0 g dietary fiber, 324 mg sodium.*

Menu suggestion: *For a just-right accompaniment, try Curry and Apricot Pilaf (see recipe, page 85).*

FLORENTINE ROTOLO

Serves 6

½ **cup all-purpose flour**
1 **egg yolk**
2 **tablespoons water**
1 **teaspoon olive oil**
2 **tablespoons all-purpose flour**
1 **10-ounce package frozen chopped spinach**
1 **tablespoon thinly sliced green onion**
1 **beaten egg**
⅓ **cup low-fat ricotta cheese**
¼ **cup freshly grated Parmesan cheese**
¼ **cup finely chopped walnuts *or* hazelnuts**
Dash *each* ground nutmeg *and* lemon-pepper seasoning
2 **cups sliced fresh mushrooms**
1 **tablespoon butter**
1 **15-ounce can tomato sauce**
1 **teaspoon sugar**
½ **teaspoon dried basil, crushed**
Dash pepper
Freshly grated Parmesan cheese

For pasta: In a bowl stir together the ½ cup flour and ¼ teaspoon *salt.* Combine egg yolk, water, and olive oil; add to flour and stir well. Sprinkle the 2 tablespoons flour on a wooden board. Knead dough on board about 8 minutes or till smooth. Cover dough lightly; let rest 10 minutes. On a lightly floured surface, roll dough to a 12-inch square. Let stand, uncovered, for 15 minutes. Meanwhile, in a very large kettle bring lightly salted water to boiling. Carefully add pasta to boiling water; simmer for 1 to 2 minutes or till done. Carefully drain pasta into a large colander. Rinse; drain well.

For filling: Cook spinach with onion according to spinach package directions; drain well, squeezing out excess liquid. Stir together spinach mixture, egg, ricotta cheese, the ¼ cup Parmesan cheese, nuts, nutmeg, and lemon-pepper seasoning.

For sauce: Cook mushrooms in butter till tender. Stir in tomato sauce, sugar, basil, and pepper; simmer for 5 minutes.

Spread pasta on a damp cloth. Let stand about 15 minutes to dry. Trim pasta to a 14x12-inch rectangle. Spread filling over pasta to within ½ inch of edges. Sprinkle with Parmesan cheese. Using the towel and starting from a short side, roll up rotolo. Place rotolo in a greased baking pan; spoon tomato sauce over. Loosely cover pan with foil. Bake in a 350° oven about 20 minutes or till hot. Slice with a serrated knife.

Per serving: *203 cal., 10 g fat (3 g sat. fat), 83 mg chol., 9 g pro., 21 g carbo., 3 g dietary fiber, 675 mg sodium.*

Want to go all out and create a multicourse dinner for friends? This perfecto pasta roll answers both your taste and time demands. You can make the rotolo and sauce a day ahead and store in the refrigerator. When serving time rolls around, spoon the sauce over the rotolo and pop it in the oven.

—Joy Taylor

PASTA PUTTANESCA

Quick and low-fat are two prerequisites in my search for tasty, pasta recipes for special midweek dinners. And, if I can add olives (one of my passions), all the better. This version of the classic Puttanesca sauce is a big hit at our house.

—Lisa Holderness-Brown

Serves 2

3 **cloves garlic, minced**
1 **tablespoon olive oil** *or* **cooking oil**
½ **of a 2-ounce can anchovy fillets (about 5 fillets), drained**
1 **28-ounce can crushed Italian-style tomatoes, undrained,** *or* **one 35-ounce can whole Italian-style tomatoes, drained and cut up**
½ **cup imported ripe olives (such as calamata), pitted and sliced, *or* pitted ripe olives, sliced**
2 **tablespoons snipped fresh basil** *or* **2 teaspoons dried basil, crushed**
2 **teaspoons capers, drained**
Dash ground red pepper
4 **ounces fusilli** *or* **fettuccine**
2 **tablespoons grated Parmesan cheese**

In a large skillet cook the garlic in hot oil till tender but not brown. Add anchovies. With a wooden spoon, mash anchovies, making a paste. Cook and stir for 3 minutes. Stir in tomatoes, olives, basil, capers, and red pepper. Simmer, uncovered, for 20 to 25 minutes or till slightly thickened, stirring occasionally.

Meanwhile, cook pasta according to package instructions; drain. Divide pasta between two dinner plates. Ladle sauce atop and sprinkle with cheese.

Per serving: *452 cal., 15 g fat (3 g sat. fat), 28 mg chol., 18 g pro., 65 g carbo., 7 g dietary fiber, 1,558 mg sodium.*

SAUSAGE EGG SCRAMBLE

Serves 10

    8 **ounces bulk pork sausage**
  ¼ **cup chopped onion**
 12 **beaten eggs**
  2 **tablespoons margarine *or* butter**
  2 **tablespoons all-purpose flour**
  ½ **teaspooon salt**
  ⅛ **teaspoon pepper**
  2 **cups milk**
  1 **cup shredded American cheese**
  1 **4-ounce can sliced mushrooms, drained**
  1 **tablespoon margarine *or* butter, melted**
1½ **cups (2 slices) soft bread crumbs**
  ⅛ **teaspoon paprika**

In a 10-inch skillet cook sausage and onion till sausage is brown and onion is tender; drain off fat. Add eggs to skillet; scramble eggs just till set. Set aside.

In a medium saucepan melt the 2 tablespoons margarine or butter; blend in flour, salt, and pepper. Add milk all at once; cook and stir over medium heat till thickened and bubbly. Add cheese; stir till melted. Fold in eggs and mushrooms. Turn mixture into a 12x7½x2-inch baking dish. Combine melted margarine or butter, bread crumbs, and paprika; sprinkle atop eggs. Cover and chill for up to 24 hours.

To serve, bake, uncovered, in 350° oven about 30 minutes or till heated through. Serve immediately.

Per serving: *278 cal., 20 g fat (7 g sat. fat), 285 mg chol., 16 g pro., 9 g carbo., 0 g dietary fiber, 661 mg sodium.*

Menu suggestion: *Warm and gooey cinnamon rolls are a wonderful treat at brunch. Fix them from scratch, or bake the refrigerated kind just before serving. A bowl of fresh fruit will color your menu. Include sliced strawberries, halved green and red grapes, orange sections, and pear wedges. Top each serving with fruit yogurt.*

I fixed this dish most recently for a brunch following my daughter's First Communion. It fit our occasion perfectly because it was made ahead, chilled, and heated right before company arrived.

—Maryellyn Krantz

SUN-DRENCHED QUICHE

I'm always looking for new brunch ideas, and the flavors of the Mediterranean are an inspiration for me. Sun-dried tomatoes and fresh basil provide just the right amount of flavor and sophistication for this colorful entrée.

—*Carol Prager*

Serves 6

1 cup all-purpose flour
½ teaspoon salt
3 tablespoons shortening
2 tablespoons butter *or* margarine
3 to 4 tablespoons ice water
3 tablespoons sliced green onion
1 tablespoon olive oil
2 cups shredded mozzarella cheese (8 ounces)
½ cup snipped fresh basil
¼ cup grated Parmesan cheese
3 tablespoons chopped sun-dried tomatoes
4 eggs
1 pint half and half *or* light cream
¼ teaspoon salt
¼ teaspoon freshly ground black pepper
Dash ground red pepper
Dash ground nutmeg

For pastry, in a large mixing bowl stir together flour and the ½ teaspoon salt. Cut in shortening and butter or margarine till mixture resembles coarse crumbs. Sprinkle on water, 1 tablespoon at a time, tossing with a fork till pastry is moist enough to hold together. Shape dough into a ball, then flatten into a disk. Wrap in plastic wrap and refrigerate for 1 hour. Roll pastry between 2 sheets of waxed paper into an 11-inch circle. Ease pastry into a 9-inch pie plate; trim and flute edge.

In a small skillet cook green onion in hot oil over medium heat about 1 minute. Spread in bottom of prepared crust. Sprinkle mozzarella cheese, basil, Parmesan cheese, and sun-dried tomatoes into crust. In a mixing bowl whisk together the eggs, half and half or light cream, salt, black pepper, red pepper, and nutmeg. Pour egg mixture evenly into crust.

Bake in a 425° oven for 15 minutes. Reduce oven temperature to 375° and bake about 25 minutes more or till filling is just set in center. Let stand for 5 to 10 minutes before cutting into wedges.

Per serving: *455 cal., 31 g fat (15 g sat. fat), 206 mg chol., 20 g pro., 24 g carbo., 2 g dietary fiber, 619 mg sodium.*

COOKING FOR FRIENDS

When it comes to fixing food for company, practice helps. Good hosts take the basics of meal planning, then add their personal touches. Also, they're well organized. Take a cue from some of these time-proven tips to make entertaining in your home a piece of cake.

Menu Planning

Of course, you want to show your guests how special they are, yet you don't want to be a slave to your kitchen. Set your menu, keeping these suggestions in mind:

1. *Consider the occasion.* What's perfect for one occasion may be inappropriate for another. A menu for a formal dinner party for six just won't work at a buffet supper for 20.
2. *Know your cooking expertise.* Plan meals around recipes you're comfortable with, but don't be afraid to add one or two simple new dishes.
3. *Get a jump on things.* Recipes that can be partially made then frozen or refrigerated are a host's lifesaver. Look for make-ahead recipes that fit your menu. Easy-to-fix and easy-to-serve foods help keep a host calm, cool, and out of the kitchen. Try to avoid fussy last-minute details that can play havoc with your cooking timetable.
4. *Know your guests' food restrictions.* If a good friend or family member needs to follow a special diet, it may be best if you invite that person at a time when you *can* tailor the menu to your guest's restrictions.
5. *Accept offers of help.* Nowadays, most guests respond with "What can I bring?" Don't be embarrassed to accept their offer; suggest that they bring an appetizer, dessert, bottle of wine, or whatever transports easily. Remember, they'll welcome your offer to help when they invite you to their home!

Food Presentation

When planning a menu, visualize how the foods will look and taste together. Select foods and garnishes (don't forget the garnishes; they're the little extras that highlight a meal!) that pleasingly complement or contrast. Take an artist's approach to menu planning to end up with a menu that *is* exciting and delicious.

1. *Combine interesting, contrasting colors in foods.* Avoid foods that are all of the same color or texture. A vegetable puree, for example, makes a good accompaniment for crisp, oven-fried chicken, but doesn't team well with creamed seafood.
2. *Consider your table setting.* If using your best china, think about what foods look best on it. Choose table linens that complement the whole setting.
3. *Make one splashy dish.* Let the others play minor, but still important, roles. Nothing upstages a menu's star more than too many showy competitors.

Your family will love the Southwest flavors in Three-Pepper Pork with Corn Pasta (page 44).

OUR FAMILIES' FAVORITE MEALS

Through the years, each of us has gathered family-favorite recipes we rely on over and over. Flip through this chapter and you'll find the recipes we turn to when we yearn for something home-style or when we don't have the time—or the energy—to try a new recipe. With choices ranging from stir-fries and casseroles to burgers and soups, our old faithfuls might become the dishes your family asks for again and again, too.

THREE-PEPPER PORK WITH CORN PASTA

Serves 4

    8 ounces lean boneless pork
    2 medium carrots, cut into thin bias slices
    1 medium onion, cut into thin wedges
    1 clove garlic, minced
    2 tablespoons margarine *or* butter
    1 small green pepper
    1 small yellow *or* red sweet pepper
    2 tablespoons all-purpose flour
    1 cup milk
    ½ cup chicken broth
    1 4-ounce can chopped green chili peppers
    4 ounces shredded Chihuahua cheese *or* Monterey Jack cheese (1 cup)
    1 recipe hot cooked Corn Pasta *or* 8 ounces fettuccine, cooked
        according to package directions
Whole chili peppers (optional)

Partially freeze pork; thinly slice into bite-size strips. In a large skillet over medium-high heat cook carrots, onion, and garlic in margarine or butter till tender. Add pork, green pepper, and yellow or red pepper; cook and stir for 2 to 3 minutes or till pork is done. Stir in flour; add milk and broth all at once. Add green chili peppers. Cook and stir till thickened and bubbly; cook 2 minutes more. Stir in cheese. Serve over hot cooked Corn Pasta or fettuccine. Garnish with whole chili peppers, if desired.

Corn Pasta: In a large mixing bowl stir together 1 cup *all-purpose flour,* 1 cup *Masa Harina tortilla flour,* and ½ teaspoon *salt.* Make a well in the center of mixture.

In a small mixing bowl combine 2 beaten *eggs,* ⅓ cup *water,* and 1 teaspoon *olive oil* or *cooking oil.* Add to flour mixture and mix well.

Sprinkle kneading surface with ⅓ cup *all-purpose flour.* Turn dough onto floured surface. Knead till dough is smooth and elastic (8 to 10 minutes). Cover and let rest 10 minutes.

Divide dough into thirds. On a lightly floured surface roll each third of dough into a ¹⁄₁₆-inch-thick rectangle (about 16x12 inches). Let stand about 20 minutes or till slightly dry. Cut into thin strips (about ¼ inch wide). Cook in lightly salted boiling water 2 to 3 minutes or just till tender. Makes about 1 pound pasta.

Per serving: *626 cal., 24 g fat (10 g sat. fat), 170 mg chol., 34 g pro., 69 g carbo., 7 g dietary fiber, 714 mg sodium.*

ISLAND TERIYAKI

Serves 6

 1½ **pounds boneless beef sirloin *or* round steak**
 ½ **cup soy sauce**
 ¼ **cup packed brown sugar**
 2 **tablespoons olive oil *or* cooking oil**
 2 **cloves garlic, minced**
 1 **teaspoon ground ginger**
 ¼ **teaspoon cracked black pepper**

Partially freeze beef; thinly slice across the grain into bite-size strips. In a plastic bag combine soy sauce, brown sugar, olive oil or cooking oil, garlic, ginger, and pepper. Add beef strips. Seal bag and marinate, chilled, for 4 hours or overnight, turning bag several times. Drain beef, discarding marinade. Thread beef onto 10-or 12-inch skewers. Cook on an uncovered grill directly over *medium-hot* coals about 10 minutes or till desired doneness, turning several times.

Per serving: *250 cal., 11 g fat (3 g sat. fat), 76 mg chol., 27 g pro., 11 g carbo., 0 g dietary fiber, 967 mg sodium.*

My family prefers beef for this grilled specialty, but a Hawaiian friend says chicken teriyaki is more common in her native state. Either way, with a little preparation the day before, it's a super-easy dish to fix after work.

—Jennifer Peterson

ONION-MUSHROOM CHARCOAL BURGERS

Serves 6 to 8

 1 **beaten egg**
 ¼ **cup fine dry bread crumbs**
 ¼ **cup catsup**
 1 **envelope *regular* onion-mushroom soup mix**
 1 **tablespoon water**
 1½ **pounds lean ground beef**
   Hamburger buns (optional)

Combine egg, bread crumbs, catsup, soup mix, and water. Add ground beef and mix well. Form into six to eight ¾-inch-thick patties. Grill over *medium* coals about 15 minutes or till done, turning once. Serve on buns, if desired.

Per serving: *214 cal., 8 g fat (3 g sat. fat), 102 mg chol., 27 g pro., 8 g carbo., 0 g dietary fiber, 597 mg sodium.*

These flavorful burgers are a hit with adults and kids alike!

—Kay Cargill

CALIFORNIA BURGERS

Serves 4

  1 pound lean ground beef
  ⅛ teaspoon salt
  ⅛ teaspoon lemon-pepper seasoning
  ¼ cup sodium-reduced soy sauce
  ¼ cup dry sherry
  1 clove garlic, minced
1½ teaspoons dry mustard
1½ teaspoons brown sugar
  ½ teaspoon ground ginger
  4 hamburger buns
  4 tomato slices
Shredded lettuce

In a medium mixing bowl combine ground beef, salt, and lemon-pepper seasoning. Shape into four ¾-inch-thick patties. Place patties in a shallow baking dish. In a bowl combine soy sauce, sherry, garlic, dry mustard, brown sugar, and ginger. Pour soy mixture over patties. Cover and refrigerate 2 to 24 hours.

To grill, remove patties from marinade. Pat dry with paper towels. Grill patties over *medium* coals about 15 minutes or till no longer pink, turning patties once. Serve the burgers on hamburger buns with tomato slices and lettuce.

Per serving: *411 cal., 11 g fat (3 g sat. fat), 66 mg chol., 32 g pro., 42 g carbo., 3 g dietary fiber, 1,071 mg sodium.*

Serving suggestion: *Round out the meal with a marinated pasta salad and sliced fresh strawberries.*

PASTA PIZZA

Serves 8

  2 **cups corkscrew macaroni**
  2 **slightly beaten eggs**
  ½ **cup milk**
  ½ **cup shredded cheddar cheese (2 ounces)**
  1 **pound lean ground beef** *or* **bulk pork sausage**
  1 **15-ounce can tomato sauce**
  2 **teaspoons dried Italian seasoning**
  ¼ **teaspoon garlic salt**
  1 **4-ounce can sliced mushrooms, drained**
  1 **medium green pepper, chopped**
1½ **cups shredded mozzarella cheese (6 ounces)**

Cook macaroni according to package directions; drain well. Combine eggs, milk, and cheddar cheese. Stir in cooked macaroni; mix well. Spread macaroni mixture evenly into a lightly greased 12-inch pizza pan that has ½-inch sides. Bake in a 350° oven for 20 minutes.

Meanwhile, in a large skillet cook ground beef or sausage till brown; drain off fat. Stir in tomato sauce, Italian seasoning, and garlic salt. Bring to boiling. Reduce heat; cover and simmer for 10 minutes. Spoon meat mixture over baked macaroni crust. Top with mushrooms and green pepper. Sprinkle with mozzarella cheese. Bake about 15 minutes more or till cheese is melted.

Per serving: *318 cal., 12 g fat (5 g sat. fat), 107 mg chol., 26 g pro., 28 g carbo., 1 g dietary fiber, 630 mg sodium.*

A weekly regular in our family, this easy-to-make dish combines both pasta and pizza—two foods we really love. Plus, the pasta crust is easier to make than traditional pizza crust.

—Lynn Blanchard

SNAPPY MEXICAN SALAD

You can call this "traveler salad"—we take it everywhere, from picnics in the park to family potlucks. I chill the prepared meat mixture in the saucepan, then tote the saucepan, lettuce, and cheese in an ice chest. When we arrive at our dining spot, I reheat the meat mixture and toss it with the lettuce, cheese, and chips.

—Jennifer Peterson

Serves 10

  1 **medium head iceberg lettuce, cut up**
  3 **cups shredded cheddar *or* Monterey Jack cheese (12 ounces)**
  1 **16-ounce package nacho-flavored tortilla chips, coarsely crushed**
1½ **pounds lean ground beef**
  1 **16-ounce can red kidney beans, drained**
 ¾ **cup French salad dressing**
 ¾ **cup water**
  1 **to 2 tablespoons chili powder**
 ½ **teaspoon salt**
 ¼ **teaspoon pepper**

In an extra-large mixing bowl toss together lettuce, cheese, and crushed tortilla chips. Set aside. In a large saucepan cook ground beef till brown; drain off fat. Stir in kidney beans, French dressing, water, chili powder, salt, and pepper. Heat through. Pour over lettuce mixture. Toss to coat. Serve immediately.

Per serving: *586 cal., 37 g fat (13 g sat. fat), 76 mg chol., 30 g pro., 41 g carbo., 6 g dietary fiber, 755 mg sodium.*

Note: *For a spicier salad, use Monterey Jack cheese with jalapeño peppers.*

ENCHILADA CASSEROLE

Serves 8

- ½ **pound ground beef**
- ½ **pound ground pork**
- 1 **medium green pepper, chopped**
- 1 **medium onion, chopped**
- 2 **cloves garlic, minced**
- 2 **cups picante sauce**
- 1 **16-ounce can pinto beans, drained**
- 1 **15-ounce can tomato sauce**
- 1 **teaspoon ground cumin**
- 12 **corn tortillas**
- 2 **cups shredded Monterey Jack *or* cheddar cheese (8 ounces)**

In a 12-inch skillet cook ground beef, ground pork, green pepper, onion, and garlic till meat is brown; drain off fat. Stir in picante sauce, pinto beans, the tomato sauce, and cumin. Cover and simmer for 15 minutes.

Spoon *one-third* of the meat-bean mixture into bottom of an ungreased 13x9x2-inch baking dish, spreading to cover. Layer 6 of the tortillas in dish, overlapping as necessary. Top with *another third* of the remaining meat-bean mixture. Sprinkle with *1 cup* of the shredded cheese. Cover with remaining tortillas, overlapping to cover cheese layer. Top with remaining meat-bean mixture. Cover and bake in a 350° oven about 20 minutes or till heated through.

Uncover; sprinkle with remaining shredded cheese. Bake for 5 minutes more. Let stand about 10 minutes before serving.

Per serving: *397 cal., 18 g fat (8 g sat. fat), 63 mg chol., 26 g pro., 39 g carbo., 10 g dietary fiber, 894 mg sodium.*

For more Southwest flavor, top this delicious Tex-Mex dish with shredded lettuce, chopped tomato, sour cream, or guacamole.

—Lois White

MEATBALLS IN CARAWAY SAUCE WITH SPAETZLE

Sixteen years ago, I first prepared this dinner for my future husband. John wasn't much of a cook (still isn't!), and he was looking forward to a homecooked meal. It's still one of his most requested meals, but these days I sometimes season the dish with dill instead of caraway to satisfy my children's tastes.

—Maryellyn Krantz

Serves 4 to 6

> 1 slightly beaten egg
> ¼ cup fine dry bread crumbs
> ¼ cup milk
> ¼ teaspoon salt
> ¼ teaspoon ground sage
> ⅛ teaspoon pepper
> 1 pound lean ground beef *or* pork
> 1 10½-ounce can condensed beef broth
> 1 4-ounce can mushroom stems and pieces
> ½ cup chopped onion
> 1 cup dairy sour cream
> 2 tablespoons all-purpose flour
> ½ teaspoon caraway seed *or* dried dillweed
> Hot cooked spaetzle *or* noodles

In a bowl combine egg, bread crumbs, milk, salt, sage, and pepper; add ground meat and mix well. Shape into 24 meatballs. In a large skillet brown meatballs, *half* at a time; drain off fat. Return all meatballs to skillet. Add broth, *undrained* mushrooms, and onion. Bring to boiling; reduce heat. Simmer, covered, for 30 minutes.

Combine sour cream, flour, and caraway seed; carefully stir into skillet. Cook and stir till mixture thickens. Serve over spaetzle or noodles.

Per serving: *481 cal., 22 g fat (11 g sat. fat), 173 mg chol., 36 g pro., 34 g carbo., 3 g dietary fiber, 930 mg sodium.*

CORNED BEEF HASH

Serves 3 or 4

        8 **ounces cooked corned beef, finely chopped**
        1 **small onion, finely chopped**
        1 **small green pepper, finely chopped**
        1 **tablespoon cooking oil**
    1½ **teaspoons Worcestershire sauce**
Dash bottled hot pepper sauce
        2 **tablespoons cooking oil**
        2 **cups refrigerated loose-pack hash brown potatoes**

In a large skillet cook corned beef, onion, and green pepper in 1 tablespoon hot oil till corned beef is lightly brown and vegetables are tender. Remove meat and vegetables from skillet; stir Worcestershire sauce and hot pepper sauce into corned beef mixture. Add the 2 tablespoons oil to the skillet. Spread potatoes evenly in skillet. Cook over medium heat about 8 minutes or till slightly browned on bottom, turning occasionally. Stir in corned beef mixture; continue cooking till potatoes are light brown and mixture is heated through.

Per serving: *388 cal., 30 g fat (7 g sat. fat), 74 mg chol., 16 g pro., 18 g carbo., 2 g dietary fiber, 926 mg sodium.*

Note: *You can use the food processor to finely chop the onion and green pepper, too.*

Even my 12-year-old-daughter Kristin shows off her cooking prowess. We frequently cook a 2- to 3-pound piece of corned beef, trim off the fat, divide the meat into 8-ounce portions, and freeze the portions in freezer bags. Then, on Kristin's night to cook, she thaws a portion of meat in the microwave and finely chops it in the food processor.

—Sharyl Heiken

ORIENTAL CHICKEN STIR-FRY

Most Western versions of Oriental recipes call for more meat than vegetables. My husband and I prefer lots of fresh vegetables, so we usually cut up any extra veggies in our refrigerator and add them to this tasty stir-fry.

—Kristi Fuller

Serves 4

- 2 boneless, skinless large chicken breast halves
- 1 egg white
- 1 tablespoon cornstarch
- 1 tablespoon sodium-reduced soy sauce
- 2 teaspoons cooking oil
- ½ cup chicken broth
- 3 tablespoons sodium-reduced soy sauce
- 1 tablespoon cornstarch
- 1 tablespoon cooking oil
- 1 to 2 tablespoons cooking oil
- 1 small onion, cut into 1-inch pieces
- 2 cloves garlic, minced
- 2 cups broccoli flowerettes
- 4 ounces fresh pea pods, cut in half, *or* one 6-ounce package frozen pea pods, thawed
- 1 medium red sweet pepper, cut in ½-inch squares
- 1 cup sliced fresh mushrooms
- 2 tablespoons hoisin sauce *or* stir-fry sauce
- ½ cup slivered almonds *or* unsalted cashew halves (optional)

Hot cooked rice

Partially freeze the chicken; thinly slice into bite-size strips. In a small bowl combine egg white, the first 1 tablespoon cornstarch, the 1 tablespoon soy sauce, and the 2 teaspoons cooking oil. Add chicken strips; toss to coat. Cover and refrigerate about 30 minutes; drain chicken strips well, discarding the egg white mixture.

In a small bowl combine chicken broth, the 3 tablespoons soy sauce, and the remaining 1 tablespoon cornstarch; set aside. In a large skillet or wok heat 1 tablespoon cooking oil over high heat. Add chicken strips; stir-fry for 2 to 3 minutes or till no longer pink. Remove chicken from skillet or wok.

Add the remaining 1 to 2 tablespoons cooking oil to skillet or wok. To the hot oil add onion and garlic; stir-fry 1 minute or till onion is tender. Add broccoli, pea pods, sweet pepper, and mushrooms. Stir-fry vegetables 2 to 3 minutes or till crisp-tender.

Stir broth mixture; add to skillet. Continue to cook vegetables till sauce thickens (about 1 minute more). Stir in cooked chicken, the hoisin sauce or stir-fry sauce, and nuts; heat through. Serve over hot cooked rice.

Per serving: *373 cal., 12 g fat (2 g sat. fat), 36 mg chol., 22 g pro., 45 g carbo., 4 g dietary fiber, 852 mg sodium.*

A bright and nutritious mix of Oriental vegetables. ▶

LEMON-DILL CHICKEN

Like other working parents, I pick up my children after work, then head right home. Once there, time is at a premium for fixing supper because my boys want dinner ASAP! If I buy boneless chicken breasts, we can have this dish ready-to-eat in only 15 minutes.

—Sandra Granseth

Serves 4

>   1 tablespoon margarine *or* butter
> 1½ teaspoons snipped fresh dillweed *or* ½ teaspoon dried dillweed
> ¼ teaspoon pepper
>   2 medium whole chicken breasts (about 1½ pounds total), skinned, boned, and cut into thin 3-inch-long strips
>   1 tablespoon lemon juice

In a 10-inch skillet melt margarine or butter. Stir in dillweed and pepper. Add chicken strips; cook and stir over medium-high heat for 5 to 6 minutes or till chicken is no longer pink.

Transfer chicken to a warm serving platter. Cover to keep warm. Reduce heat, then carefully add lemon juice to skillet. Heat and stir, scraping up browned bits. Spoon lemon juice mixture over chicken.

Per serving: *137 cal., 6 g fat (1 g sat. fat), 54 mg chol., 20 g pro., 1 g carbo., 0 g dietary fiber, 83 mg sodium.*

Serving suggestion: *Hot cooked rice and steamed broccoli spears are great complements to this tangy chicken.*

TURKEY RICOTTA BAKE

Serves 6

1 10-ounce package frozen chopped spinach
3 beaten eggs
1 15-ounce carton ricotta cheese
1 cup fine dry bread crumbs
½ cup grated Parmesan cheese
¼ teaspoon salt
1 pound ground turkey
1 8-ounce can tomato sauce
1 tablespoon all-purpose flour
1 teaspoon dried oregano, crushed
½ teaspoon garlic powder
¼ cup fine dry bread crumbs

Cook spinach according to package directions; drain and squeeze dry. In a large mixing bowl stir together eggs, spinach, ricotta, the 1 cup bread crumbs, the Parmesan cheese, and salt. Set aside.

In skillet cook turkey till brown; drain off fat. Stir tomato sauce, flour, oregano, and garlic powder into skillet.

Layer *half* of the ricotta mixture in a greased 8x8x2-inch baking pan. Spread turkey mixture over; top with remaining ricotta mixture. Sprinkle with the ¼ cup bread crumbs. Bake in a 350° oven for 30 to 35 minutes or till hot. Serve immediately.

Per serving: *443 cal., 23 g fat (10 g sat. fat), 193 mg chol., 34 g pro., 25 g carbo., 3 g dietary fiber, 788 mg sodium.*

Serving suggestion: *Drizzle tomato and cucumber slices with a tangy, no-oil Italian salad dressing for a healthful salad accompaniment.*

If you want to reduce the fat in this cheese-rich dish, substitute low-fat cottage cheese for the ricotta. Also, for the leanest turkey, ask your butcher to grind a turkey breast without the skin.

—Patty Beebout

MUSHROOM AND HAM LASAGNA

When my husband, David, and I both worked for the same company, we each brought home a 5-pound canned ham at holiday time. What does a two-person household do with 10 pounds of ham? We became very creative in using up the ham! But this recipe is one we always come back to. Many friends and family have enjoyed it and request it whenever they know we have stockpiled some ham!

—Joy Taylor

Serves 4 to 6

  9 **lasagna noodles**
  1 **15-ounce carton low-fat ricotta cheese**
  ¼ **cup milk**
Dash pepper
Nonstick spray coating
  1 **8-ounce carton fresh mushrooms, sliced**
  4 to 6 **green onions, sliced**
  1 **14½-ounce can chunky-style stewed tomatoes**
  1 **cup ham cut into bite-size strips**
  ¼ **cup dry white wine**
  ½ **teaspoon dried basil, crushed**
  ¼ **teaspoon dried oregano, crushed**
  ⅓ **cup freshly grated Parmesan cheese**

Cook lasagna noodles in boiling unsalted water according to package directions. Drain, rinse, and drain again; set aside. In a medium mixing bowl combine the ricotta cheese, milk, and pepper.

Spray a large skillet with nonstick coating; cook the mushrooms and onions till almost tender. Add the *undrained* tomatoes, ham, wine, basil, and oregano. Simmer, uncovered, about 5 minutes to evaporate some of the liquid.

Spray an 8x8x2-inch baking pan with nonstick coating. Arrange a single layer of lasagna noodles in bottom of pan. Spread with *one-third* of the ricotta mixture, *one-third* of the mushroom mixture, and some of the Parmesan cheese. Repeat layers twice more, ending with Parmesan cheese. Cover with foil. Bake in a 350° oven about 40 minutes or till heated through.

Per serving: *484 cal., 14 g fat (7 g sat. fat), 59 mg chol., 33 g pro., 53 g carbo., 3 g dietary fiber, 987 mg sodium.*

THREE-CHEESE-STUFFED SHELLS

Serves 4

> 8 packaged jumbo pasta shells
> 1 beaten egg
> 1 cup low-fat cottage cheese, drained
> ½ cup shredded mozzarella cheese (2 ounces)
> ½ cup grated Parmesan cheese
> 2 tablespoons snipped parsley
> ½ teaspoon dried oregano, crushed
> 1 10-ounce can tomatoes and green chili peppers
> 2 teaspoons cornstarch

Cook pasta according to package directions. Drain well. In a medium mixing bowl stir together egg, cottage cheese, mozzarella cheese, Parmesan cheese, parsley, and oregano. Spoon about *¼ cup* cheese mixture into each shell; place shells in a 10x6x2-inch baking dish.

In a small saucepan combine *undrained* tomatoes and cornstarch. Cook and stir over medium heat till slightly thickened and bubbly. Cook and stir 2 minutes more. Pour over shells in baking dish. Bake in a 350° oven for 25 to 30 minutes or till hot.

Per serving: *246 cal., 8 g fat (4 g sat. fat), 74 mg chol., 20 g pro., 22 g carbo., 0 g dietary fiber, 784 mg sodium.*

Note: *If you can't find the jumbo shells, substitute manicotti shells but plan on needing a little more time to fill the manicotti.*

Jumbo pasta shells are a cinch to fill—just gently nestle a shell in your hand and spoon in the cheese filling. Even young children can handle the job!

—Janet Figg

PIZZA CASSEROLE

My mother-in-law shared this recipe with me 20 years ago. Today, it is one of the most frequently asked for meals at our house.

—Judy Comstock

Serves 8

> **10** **ounces medium noodles**
> **¾** **pound bulk Italian sausage**
> **1** **15-ounce can tomato sauce**
> **1** **8-ounce can tomato sauce**
> **1** **8-ounce package (2 cups) shredded mozzarella cheese**
> **½** **of a 10¾-ounce can condensed cream of mushroom soup**
> **1** **3½-ounce package sliced pepperoni**
> **1** **2½-ounce jar sliced mushrooms, drained**
> **1** **2¼-ounce can sliced pitted ripe olives, drained**
> **1½** **teaspoons pizza seasoning *or* dried Italian seasoning, crushed**
> **⅛** **teaspoon garlic powder**

Cook noodles according to package directions. Drain.

Meanwhile, in a medium skillet cook Italian sausage till brown. Drain off fat. In a 13x9x2-inch baking dish combine noodles, Italian sausage, tomato sauce, *half* of the mozzarella cheese, the mushroom soup, pepperoni, mushrooms, olives, pizza seasoning or Italian seasoning, and garlic powder. Mix well. Sprinkle with remaining mozzarella cheese. Bake in a 350° oven for 45 minutes or till heated through.

Per serving: *417 cal., 22 g fat (8 g sat. fat), 99 mg chol., 22 g pro., 35 g carbo., 2 g dietary fiber, 1,402 mg sodium.*

Note: *If you want to cut the amount of sodium in each serving, use low-salt tomato sauce and condensed soup.*

CURRIED SAUSAGE-STUFFED SQUASH

Serves 4

2 medium acorn squash
1¼ cups chicken broth
½ cup regular brown rice
½ cup mixed dried fruit bits
1 pound bulk pork sausage
½ cup chopped onion
½ cup chutney
2 to 3 teaspoons curry powder
¼ cup chopped peanuts

Halve squash; remove seeds. Bake, cut side down, in a shallow baking pan in a 350° oven for 50 minutes or till tender.

Meanwhile, in a small saucepan combine broth, rice, and fruit bits. Bring to boiling; reduce heat and simmer, covered, for 40 to 50 minutes or till rice is tender. In a large skillet cook sausage and onion till meat is brown and onion is tender. Drain off fat. Stir chutney and curry powder into sausage mixture; heat through. Stir in cooked rice mixture and the peanuts. Mound sausage mixture into squash halves. Return the stuffed squash to the shallow baking pan. Cover with foil. Bake in a 350° oven for 20 to 25 minutes or till heated through.

Per serving: *677 cal., 30 g fat (9 g sat. fat), 64 mg chol., 24 g pro., 81 g carbo., 6 g dietary fiber, 1,640 mg sodium.*

You can make this hearty dish the night before serving. Just cover and chill the stuffed squash. Then, bake it for 40 to 45 minutes or till heated through.

—Sharon Stilwell

RED BEANS AND RICE

Serves 8

1 pound dry red kidney beans (2½ cups)
6 cups water
2 pounds fully cooked smoked pork sausage links, cut into 1-inch-thick slices
1 cup cubed fully cooked ham
1 large onion, chopped
2 cloves garlic, minced
1 bay leaf
1 teaspoon Worcestershire sauce
½ teaspoon bottled hot pepper sauce
¼ teaspoon salt
4 cups hot cooked rice

Rinse dry red kidney beans. In a large kettle or Dutch oven combine beans and water. Bring to boiling; reduce heat. Simmer, uncovered, for 2 minutes. Remove from heat. Cover; let stand for 1 hour. (*Or,* to skip boiling the water, soak beans overnight in a covered pan.)

Drain beans in a colander and rinse. In the same kettle or Dutch oven combine beans, 6 cups *fresh water,* sausage, ham, onion, garlic, bay leaf, Worcestershire sauce, hot pepper sauce, and salt. Bring to boiling; cover and simmer about 2½ hours or till beans are tender, stirring occasionally and adding more water if necessary.

To thicken, if desired, remove *1 cup* beans with a slotted spoon and mash; stir into remaining beans. Simmer, uncovered, about 15 minutes more or till desired consistency. Remove bay leaf before serving. Serve over rice.

Per serving: *661 cal., 27 g fat (9 g sat. fat), 62 mg chol., 38 g pro., 67 g carbo., 13 g dietary fiber, 1,487 mg sodium.*

BROCCOLI-BRATWURST SOUP

Serves 3

- 1 10¾-ounce can condensed cream of broccoli soup
- 1 soup can milk
- ½ teaspoon dried thyme, crushed
- 1 10-ounce package frozen mixed vegetables (New England style)
- 1 to 2 fully cooked smoked bratwurst, cut in bite-size pieces
- ½ cup shredded cheddar cheese (2 ounces)

In a saucepan combine soup, milk, and thyme. Bring to boiling; reduce heat. Stir in vegetables and bratwurst. Simmer, covered, 8 minutes. Top each serving with cheese.

Per serving: *368 cal., 23 g fat (11 g sat. fat), 54 mg chol., 16 g pro., 27 g carbo., 2 g dietary fiber, 1,313 mg sodium.*

You can't miss with this quick pantry dinner. If you keep bite-size pieces of bratwurst in your freezer (like I do), you'll need to lengthen the cooking time a few minutes to get the sausage heated through.

—Diane Yanney

MAKE-AHEAD MINESTRONE

Serves 8 to 10

- 3 14½-ounce cans beef broth
- 1 12-ounce can vegetable juice cocktail
- 1 6-ounce can Italian-style tomato paste
- 1 tablespoon Kitchen Bouquet
- 2 teaspoons sugar
- 1 16-ounce can Italian-style stewed tomatoes
- 1 15-ounce can kidney beans, drained
- 1 15-ounce can garbanzo beans, drained
- 2 cups torn fresh spinach
- 1½ cups loose-pack frozen mixed vegetables (corn, green beans, carrots)
- 2 cups cooked pasta (such as shells or tiny bow ties)

In a large Dutch oven combine broth, vegetable juice, tomato paste, Kitchen Bouquet, sugar, tomatoes, and beans. Bring to boiling. Add spinach and mixed vegetables. Reduce heat; simmer, covered, 10 minutes. Remove from heat; cool. Refrigerate, covered, overnight. To serve, reheat soup over medium heat. Stir in cooked pasta; heat through. Sprinkle each serving with *Parmesan cheese,* if desired.

Per serving: *232 cal., 2 g fat (0 g sat. fat), 0 mg chol., 13 g pro., 44 g carbo., 9 g dietary fiber, 1,183 mg sodium.*

For best flavors, prepare this soup the night before serving. You'll appreciate the convenience of a quick-to-reheat meal, and the soup tastes better because the flavors have had a chance to blend.

—Kristi Fuller

MIXED BEAN SOUP

Serves 4

> 1 **cup dry beans (such as pinto, kidney, garbanzo,**
>   **great northern, *and/or* green split peas)**
> 4 **cups water**
> 1½ **cups sliced celery**
> 1½ **cups chopped onion**
> 1 **cup chopped carrot**
> 1 **teaspoon dried thyme, crushed**
> ¼ **teaspoon salt**
> ¼ **teaspoon pepper**
> 1 **bay leaf**
> 4 **ounces fully cooked ham, diced**
> 1 **16-ounce can stewed tomatoes**

Rinse beans. In a large saucepan combine beans and water. Bring to boiling; reduce heat. Simmer for 2 minutes. Remove from heat. Cover and let stand for 1 hour. (*Or,* to skip boiling the water, soak beans overnight in a covered pan.) Drain and rinse beans. In the same pan combine beans, 4 cups *fresh water,* the celery, onion, carrot, thyme, salt, pepper, and bay leaf. Bring to boiling; reduce heat. Cover; simmer about 1 hour or till beans are tender. Stir in ham and stewed tomatoes. Heat through. Remove bay leaf before serving.

Per serving: *278 cal., 2 g fat (1 g sat. fat), 16 mg chol., 20 g pro., 47 g carbo., 15 g dietary fiber, 870 mg sodium.*

Note: *Buy whatever dry beans, split peas, or lentils you find when shopping, then mix them all together and store them in plastic bags. (If you use black beans in the mixture, expect a muddy-colored soup.)*

Serve your family a hearty soup on chilly days. ▶

SPLIT PEA SOUP

Soup's always a winner at our house, so I never make less than a potful at a time. If any of this old-fashioned meatless soup is left over, it freezes well.

—Janet Figg

Serves 8

1 16-ounce package dry split peas
9 cups water
2 tablespoons instant chicken bouillon granules
1 clove garlic, minced
1 teaspoon dried Italian seasoning, crushed
¼ teaspoon pepper
2 medium carrots, sliced (1 cup)
2 stalks celery, sliced (1 cup)
1 large onion, chopped (1 cup)
1 small turnip, chopped (¾ cup)

Rinse the split peas. In a Dutch oven combine peas, water, instant bouillon granules, minced garlic, Italian seasoning, and pepper. Bring mixture to boiling; reduce heat. Cover and simmer for 1 hour.

Stir in the carrots, celery, onion, and turnip. Return to boiling; reduce heat. Cover and simmer about 30 minutes more or till all of the vegetables are tender.

Per serving: *227 cal., 1 g fat (0 g sat. fat), 0 mg chol., 15 g pro., 41 g carbo., 9 g dietary fiber, 719 mg sodium.*

Serving suggestion: *Complement this flavorful soup with ham or smoked turkey sandwiches and crisp apples.*

MAKING THE MOST OF FAMILY MEALTIMES

Family mealtime is a lot more than just the food you eat. At its best, meals should be a blend of good food, lively conversation, and family togetherness. It is a prime time for families to share experiences and show loving support. To make the most of breakfast, lunch, and dinner at your house, plan first, then get ready to gather round the table.

Before the Meal

A relaxed, loving dinner routine is more than a matter of luck; it takes smart planning by cooks to bring off enjoyable times at the dining table. Try some of the following tips to help set the scene.

1. *Have a regularly scheduled dinner* and stress the importance for everyone to set aside at least half an hour for the meal. If it's impossible to eat together every night of the week, designate certain nights "family nights." Make it a house rule that on these nights everyone must be home for dinner.
2. *Do some of the food preparation ahead*—on weekends, the evening before, or earlier in the day. Look for recipes you can prepare ahead, then refrigerate or freeze to serve later. With this type of a head start, you can avoid a lot of hectic, last-minute desperation preparation. You and your family will start the meal relaxed and ready to talk and listen.
3. *If time is at a premium, keep the cooking simple*—an easy main dish plus a salad or vegetable—to make sure you can devote time to conversation.
4. *Pick up dinner* at the deli or other favorite take-out shop when you don't feel like cooking at all.
5. *Involve all family members* in preparing the meal, and use this time to talk over the day's happenings.

At the Table

Once the food is on the table, turn your attention to each other. Remember these hints to spur discussion and make the occasion enjoyable for everyone.

1. *Keep the conversation pleasant.* Avoid bringing up problems or making negative comments (including comments on poor etiquette). Look for positive topics to discuss.
2. *Get the children involved in the conversation.* Ask them about what they did that day, then listen to their answer. Ask some follow-up questions, too. If the response is "Not much" or the children resent your "nosiness," tell something about your day to try to draw them out.
3. *Share an item of mutual interest* such as a letter, newspaper clipping, magazine article, or photograph with the family. This can lead to a lively discussion of world events, family plans, or even personal hopes and dreams.

Fresh and easy—Greens with Honey-Mustard Dressing (page 68) with Toasted Parmesan Bread (page 103).

ON THE SIDE

For all cooks—beginners and experts alike—the easiest part of menu planning is selecting a main dish. After that, the choices get tougher: What will accent the flavor of grilled fish? What can spiff up a basic lettuce salad? How can you fix the veggies so the kids will eat them?

Turn the page and uncover a treasury of our favorite meal accompaniments. Choose a salad, soup, vegetable, or pasta dish from this savory sampling to round out a meal with homemade goodness.

GREENS WITH HONEY-MUSTARD DRESSING

For dressing with a kick, sprinkle a drop or two of bottled hot pepper sauce in the dressing before shaking.

—*Diane Yanney*

Serves 4

    4 **cups torn mixed greens**
    1 **medium yellow *and/or* red tomato, cut into thin wedges**
    3 **cups sliced fresh mushrooms**
    3 **tablespoons vinegar**
    2 **tablespoons salad oil**
    1 **tablespoon country-style Dijon mustard**
    1 **tablespoon honey**
Edible flowers (optional)

In a large salad bowl combine the mixed greens, tomato wedges, and mushrooms. Set aside.

For dressing, in a screw-top jar combine the vinegar, salad oil, country-style mustard, and honey. Cover and shake well. Pour over the greens and vegetable mixture. Toss well to coat. If desired, garnish with edible flowers.

Per serving: *167 cal., 13 g fat (2 g sat.), 0 mg chol., 6 g pro., 13 g carbo., 2 g dietary fiber, 127 mg sodium.*

Editor's note: *For a special touch, sprinkle ¼ cup toasted pine nuts over the salad. To toast the pine nuts, spread them into a thin layer in a shallow baking pan. Bake in a 350° oven for 5 to 10 minutes or till light golden brown, stirring once or twice.*

SPINACH SALAD WITH GLAZED ALMONDS

Serves 6

   ¼ **cup sugar**
   ¾ **cup sliced almonds**
   6 **cups torn fresh spinach *or* torn mixed greens**
   2 **medium oranges, peeled and sectioned, *or* one 11-ounce can**
       mandarin orange sections, drained
   1 **small red *or* yellow onion, thinly sliced and separated into rings**
   ¼ **cup oil-free clear Italian salad dressing**

For glazed almonds, place the sugar in a heavy small skillet or saucepan. Heat over medium-high heat, without stirring, till the sugar begins to melt, shaking skillet occasionally to heat sugar evenly. Reduce heat to low; add the almonds. Cook, stirring constantly, till the sugar is golden brown and completely melted. Immediately turn the glazed almonds out onto buttered foil to cool. Break into small clusters.

In a large salad bowl combine the torn spinach or mixed greens, orange sections, onion rings, and glazed almonds. Drizzle with the salad dressing. Toss gently to coat.

Per serving: *183 cal., 12 g fat (1 g sat.), 0 mg chol., 5 g pro., 20 g carbo., 5 g dietary fiber, 123 mg sodium.*

Editor's note: *For mixed salad greens, combine equal amounts of mild-flavored greens, such as iceberg lettuce, romaine, curly endive, Belgian endive, or leaf lettuce, with a strong-flavored green like mustard greens, beet greens, or kale.*

Mixed greens, juicy oranges, and sugar-coated almonds make a mouth-watering combination. This is one salad recipe that dinner guests always request!

—Sharyl Heiken

CITRUS-GREEN SALAD

As a younger and much pickier eater, I couldn't figure out what my grandmother and mother found so glorious about the combination of citrus and red onion. Now I love it, too!

—Lisa Kingsley

Serves 6

2 large oranges, peeled and sectioned
1 medium grapefruit, peeled, sectioned, and cut into 1-inch pieces
¼ cup orange juice
1 tablespoon honey
1 teaspoon ground cinnamon
½ cup coarsely chopped walnuts
6 cups torn fresh spinach *or* torn mixed greens
½ of a small red onion, thinly sliced and separated into rings
½ cup thinly sliced radishes
½ cup raisins
2 tablespoons olive oil
Salt
Pepper

In a medium mixing bowl toss together the oranges, grapefruit, orange juice, honey, and cinnamon. Cover and chill for 1 to 4 hours.

Meanwhile, to toast the walnuts, spread the nuts into a thin layer in a shallow baking pan. Bake in a 350° oven for 5 to 10 minutes or till light brown, stirring once or twice.

At serving time, in a large salad bowl combine the orange and grapefruit mixture, toasted walnuts, torn spinach or mixed greens, red onion, radishes, raisins, and olive oil. Sprinkle with salt and pepper to taste. Toss to mix.

Per serving: *198 cal., 10 g fat (1 g sat.), 0 mg chol., 3 g pro., 28 g carbo., 4 g dietary fiber, 43 mg sodium.*

COTTAGE CHEESE-SPINACH SALAD

Serves 6 to 8

　　7　cups torn fresh spinach
1½　cups cream-style cottage cheese
　½　cup chopped walnuts, toasted
　½　cup dairy sour cream
　2　tablespoons sugar
　1　tablespoon prepared horseradish
　½　teaspoon dry mustard
　3　tablespoons herb-flavored vinegar *or* white wine vinegar

In a large salad bowl arrange the torn spinach. Top with the cottage cheese and toasted walnuts. Set aside.

For dressing, in a small mixing bowl stir together the sour cream, sugar, prepared horseradish, and dry mustard. Gradually add the herb-flavored vinegar, mixing well to blend. Pour dressing over spinach and cottage cheese. Toss lightly to coat.

Per serving: *197 cal., 13 g fat (5 g sat.), 17 mg chol., 11 g pro., 11 g carbo., 3 g dietary fiber, 297 mg sodium.*

This old-fashioned salad is one I always come back to for a crowd pleaser. There's just something about the combination of greens, cottage cheese, nuts, and horseradish that delights and satisfies. For a lighter salad, use low-fat sour cream and low-fat cottage cheese.

—Marilyn Cornelius

FRESH CRANBERRY RELISH

Serves 10

　½　cup sugar
　1　teaspoon finely shredded orange peel
　¼　cup orange juice
　½　teaspoon ground cinnamon
Dash ground cloves
　3　cups cranberries
　½　cup raisins
　½　cup chopped walnuts

In a saucepan combine the sugar, orange peel and juice, cinnamon, cloves, and ½ cup *water*. Stir over low heat till sugar is dissolved. Add cranberries and raisins. Cook and stir till cranberries pop. Stir in nuts. Transfer to a bowl; cool. Cover and chill.

Per serving (¼ cup): *65 cal., 0 g fat (0 g sat.), 0 mg chol., 0 g pro., 20 g carbo., 2 g dietary fiber, 2 mg sodium.*

Growing up, my job every Thanksgiving Eve was to make the fresh cranberry relish. Like most novice cooks, I strictly followed the directions on the cranberry bag. Through the years, I've jazzed up that basic recipe to create a tastier cranberry relish for our Thanksgiving dinner.

—Joy Taylor

COUSCOUS AND BEAN SALAD

Serves 6

½ **cup water**
½ **teaspoon instant chicken bouillon granules**
 1 **cup couscous**
¼ **cup olive oil** *or* **salad oil**
 3 **tablespoons white wine vinegar**
½ **teaspoon lemon-pepper seasoning**
 2 **cloves garlic, minced,** *or* ¼ **teaspoon garlic powder**
 1 **19-ounce can fava beans** *or* **one 16-ounce can black, kidney, or pinto beans, rinsed and drained**
½ **cup coarsely chopped red** *or* **green sweet pepper**
½ **cup thinly sliced carrot**
 3 **tablespoons snipped parsley**
 2 **tablespoons chopped red onion**
 1 **small avocado** *or* **tomato (optional)**

In a medium saucepan combine the water and chicken bouillon granules. Bring to boiling; add couscous. Remove from heat. Cover and let stand for 3 to 5 minutes or till liquid is absorbed.

Meanwhile, for dressing, in a small bowl combine the olive oil or salad oil, wine vinegar, lemon-pepper seasoning, and garlic; set aside.

In a large salad bowl combine the couscous, beans, red or green pepper, carrot, parsley, and red onion. Add the dressing. Toss to coat well. Cover and refrigerate for 4 to 24 hours, stirring occasionally. If desired, just before serving, seed, peel, and cube the avocado or chop the tomato; sprinkle over the top of the salad.

Per serving: *252 cal., 9 g fat (1 g sat.), 0 mg chol., 8 g pro., 35 g carbo., 1 g dietary fiber, 161 mg sodium.*

Editor's note: *Couscous is a a pasta product that looks a bit like tiny rice and is common in North African cooking. Look for it near the rice or pasta at your supermarket or specialty food store.*

SESAME AND PEA POD PASTA SALAD

Serves 6

4 ounces linguine *or* spaghetti
2 tablespoons sesame seed
1 cup sliced fresh mushrooms
6 cherry tomatoes, halved
¼ cup sliced green onion
2 tablespoons salad oil
2 tablespoons lemon juice
2 tablespoons soy sauce
1 teaspoon grated gingerroot
1 clove garlic, minced
Few drops bottled hot pepper sauce
1 6-ounce package frozen pea pods, thawed
1 tablespoon snipped parsley *or* cilantro (optional)

Cook pasta according to package directions. Immediately drain. Rinse with cold water, then drain well.

Meanwhile, to toast the sesame seed, spread the sesame seed into a thin layer in a shallow baking pan. Bake in a 350° oven about 5 minutes or till light golden brown, stirring once or twice. Set aside.

In a large salad bowl combine the cooked linguine or spaghetti, mushrooms, cherry tomatoes, and green onion.

For dressing, in a screw-top jar combine the salad oil, lemon juice, soy sauce, gingerroot, garlic, and hot pepper sauce. Cover and shake well. Pour the dressing over the pasta and vegetable mixture. Toss to coat. Cover and refrigerate for 3 to 24 hours, stirring occasionally.

Just before serving, add the thawed pea pods. Toss pasta mixture well. Sprinkle with the toasted sesame seed and, if desired, the parsley or cilantro.

Per serving: *157 cal., 7 g fat (1 g sat.), 4 mg chol., 5 g pro., 20 g carbo., 2 g dietary fiber, 349 mg sodium.*

When it's warm, sunny, and time for outdoor cooking, it's also salad season. Remember this refreshing side dish next time you grill out.

—Lois White

OVERNIGHT PASTA SALAD

Because I live on a farm
and our dinner schedule
varies from night to
night, I always keep
dinner accompaniments
in the refrigerator, ready
for my family to eat at
any hour. This salad is
similar to a chef salad,
but is made a day
ahead.

—Patty Beebout

Serves 6 to 8

> 1 cup small shell macaroni (4 ounces)
> 2 cups shredded lettuce
> 2 hard-cooked eggs, sliced
> 1 cup fully cooked ham cut into julienne strips
> 1 cup loose-pack frozen peas, thawed
> ½ cup shredded Swiss cheese (2 ounces)
> ½ cup salad dressing
> ¼ cup plain low-fat yogurt
> 1 tablespoon chopped green onion
> 1 teaspoon prepared mustard
> Few drops bottled hot pepper sauce
> Snipped parsley

Cook the macaroni according to package directions. Immediately drain. Rinse with cold water and drain again.

Place the shredded lettuce in the bottom of a 2-quart casserole. Layer the cooked macaroni, egg slices, ham strips, peas, and Swiss cheese on top.

In a small mixing bowl stir together the salad dressing, yogurt, green onion, mustard, and hot pepper sauce. Spread dressing evenly over the top of salad, sealing to the edge of the casserole. Cover and refrigerate for 24 hours. Before serving, sprinkle with parsley; toss salad gently.

Per serving: *272 cal., 13 g fat (4 g sat.), 98 mg chol., 15 g pro., 24 g carbo., 2 g dietary fiber, 542 mg sodium.*

MARINATED ZUCCHINI SALAD

Serves 4 to 6

> 2 medium zucchini, sliced ¼ inch thick
> 2 tomatoes, cut into wedges
> 1 small onion, thinly sliced and separated into rings
> 1 small green pepper, cut into strips
> ⅔ cup vinegar
> ½ cup sugar
> ¼ cup salad oil
> ½ teaspoon celery seed

In a large salad bowl combine the zucchini slices, tomato wedges, onion rings, and pepper strips. For dressing, in a screw-top jar combine the vinegar, sugar, salad oil, celery seed, ½ teaspoon *salt,* and ⅛ teaspoon *pepper.* Cover and shake well. Pour dressing over the vegetables. Toss to coat. Cover and chill for 4 to 24 hours, stirring occasionally. Serve using a slotted spoon.

Per serving: 141 cal., 7 g fat (1 g sat.), 0 mg chol., 1 g pro., 20 g carbo., 2 g dietary fiber, 141 mg sodium.

Several years ago, a friend shared this recipe with me. Now, when the zucchini crop reaches its summer peak, this easy salad helps me use the plentiful squash deliciously.

—Kay Cargill

TOMATOES WITH BASIL VINAIGRETTE

Serves 4

> 2 medium tomatoes, cored and thinly sliced
> Lettuce leaves
> 2 tablespoons olive oil
> 1 tablespoon balsamic vinegar *or* 2 teaspoons cider vinegar
> 1 tablespoon snipped fresh basil
> 1 small clove garlic, minced

Arrange the tomatoes in a single layer on a lettuce-lined serving platter. For dressing, in a small bowl stir together the olive oil, vinegar, basil, garlic, and ⅛ teaspoon *salt.* Spoon a little dressing over each tomato slice, spreading evenly to coat. Let stand at room temperature for 30 minutes or cover and chill for up to 4 hours. Before serving, sprinkle with fresh ground *pepper.*

Per serving: 75 cal., 7 g fat (1 g sat.), 0 mg chol., 1 g pro., 4 g carbo., 1 g dietary fiber, 73 mg sodium.

Since gardening and cooking are my favorite hobbies, guests at my house usually expect something freshly made. In the heat of the summer, I know they'll always be pleased with these fresh tomatoes topped with an herb dressing.

—Sharon Stilwell

MUSHROOM BARLEY SOUP

Serves 4 to 6

5 cups beef broth
1 cup quick-cooking barley
½ cup chopped onion
2 cloves garlic, minced
1 teaspoon dried basil, crushed
1 teaspoon Worcestershire sauce
2 cups sliced fresh mushrooms
¾ cup shredded carrot
2 tablespoons cornstarch
2 tablespoons water
1 tablespoon snipped parsley

In a large saucepan bring the beef broth to boiling. Add the barley, onion, garlic, basil, and Worcestershire sauce. Reduce heat. Cover and simmer for 10 minutes or till the barley is nearly tender. Add the mushrooms and carrot. Cover and simmer for 5 minutes more.

In a small bowl combine the cornstarch and water. Add the cornstarch mixture to the saucepan. Bring mixture to boiling. Cook and stir till thickened and bubbly. Cook and stir for 2 minutes more. Stir in the parsley. To serve, ladle into soup bowls.

Per serving: *174 cal., 2 g fat (0 g sat.), 1 mg chol., 9 g pro., 37 g carbo., 6 g dietary fiber, 1,001 mg sodium.*

SAUCEPAN 'BAKED' BEANS DELUXE

Serves 16 to 20

1½ **cups chopped onion**
6 **slices bacon, cut up**
2 **16-ounce cans pork and beans with tomato sauce**
1 **15½-ounce can red kidney beans, drained**
1 **15-ounce can great northern beans, drained**
1 **15-ounce can lima beans, drained**
1 **15-ounce can butter beans, drained**
1 **15-ounce can garbanzo beans, drained**
1 **cup catsup**
⅔ **cup molasses**
¼ **cup packed brown sugar**
2 **tablespoons bottled barbecue sauce**
1 **tablespoon prepared mustard**

In a 4-quart Dutch oven cook onion and bacon till bacon is crisp and onion is tender but not brown. Drain off fat. Add the pork and beans, kidney beans, great northern beans, lima beans, butter beans, garbanzo beans, catsup, molasses, brown sugar, barbecue sauce, and mustard. Stir till combined. Cover and cook over low heat till bubbly; uncover and cook for 5 to 10 minutes more or till desired sauciness, stirring occasionally.

Per serving: *244 cal., 3 g fat (1 g sat.), 6 mg chol., 11 g pro., 47 g carbo., 11 g dietary fiber, 656 mg sodium.*

Editor's note: *The canned pork and beans are the foundation of this recipe. For the other beans in the recipe, however, feel free to mix and match to suit your whim. Just be sure to use a total of five cans beans plus the two cans of pork and beans.*

These beans make a wonderful take-along for potlucks. You can put the hot beans into a slow-electric crockery cooker and plug the cooker in as soon as you get to the party. The cooker keeps the beans hot while doubling as a serving container.

—*Sharyl Heiken*

OVEN-ROASTED GREEK VEGETABLES

Serves 6

    4 medium potatoes, cubed
    1 large onion, cut into chunks
    1 cup baby carrots, peeled and trimmed
    ⅓ cup lemon juice
    ⅓ cup olive oil
    2 cloves garlic, minced
    2 teaspoons salt
 1½ teaspoons dried oregano, crushed
    ½ teaspoon dried rosemary, crushed
    ½ teaspoon pepper
    3 cups hot water

In a greased 13x9x2-inch roasting pan combine the potatoes, onion, and carrots. Set aside.

In a small mixing bowl stir together the lemon juice, olive oil, garlic, salt, oregano, rosemary, and pepper. Drizzle over the vegetables. Toss to coat. Add the hot water. Bake, uncovered, in a 475° oven for 1 to 1¼ hours or till the vegetables are tender, stirring every 20 minutes. If necessary, add a few tablespoons water to prevent the vegetables from burning.

Per serving: *273 cal., 12 g fat (2 g sat.), 0 mg chol., 4 g pro., 39 g carbo., 5 g dietary fiber, 740 mg sodium.*

Editor's note: *Fresh lemon juice is worth the extra effort. To get ⅓ cup of juice, you'll need to squeeze two lemons.*

Sometimes the tantalizing smells coming from your oven draw people to your kitchen just as readily as the promise of what awaits them for dinner. Such is the case with Oven-Roasted Greek Vegetables. They beat a plain baked potato hands down.

—Lisa Kingsley

◀ *A hearty, country-style vegetable dish seasoned with olive oil, garlic, rosemary, and oregano.*

GINGERED BABY CARROTS

Serves 4 to 6

4 cups baby carrots, peeled and trimmed
1 1-inch piece fresh gingerroot
1 tablespoon margarine *or* butter
1 tablespoon brown sugar
1 teaspoon cornstarch
1 teaspoon finely shredded orange peel
2 teaspoons soy sauce
½ teaspoon orange juice

Cook carrots in a small amount of lightly salted boiling water for 7 to 9 minutes or till crisp-tender. Drain. Meanwhile, cut gingerroot into thin slices, then into thin strips. In a medium skillet cook gingerroot in margarine 2 minutes, stirring constantly. Stir in brown sugar, cornstarch, and orange peel. Add soy sauce and orange juice. Cook and stir till thickened and bubbly. Add carrots. Cook and stir 2 minutes more.

Per serving: *121 cal., 3 g fat (1 g sat.), 0 mg chol., 2 g pro., 23 g carbo., 6 g dietary fiber, 266 mg sodium.*

One evening, I realized my beef roast would be coming out of the oven in a matter of minutes and I hadn't started fixing a vegetable dish yet. To perk up the rather plain roast, I created these carrots, with golden orange color and spicy ginger flavor. And it worked wonderfully!

—Janet Herwig

CORN-MUSHROOM BAKE

Serves 6 to 8

1 17-ounce can cream-style corn
¼ cup all-purpose flour
1 3-ounce package cream cheese, cut into cubes
½ teaspoon onion powder
1 17-ounce can whole kernel corn, drained
1 4-ounce can mushroom stems and pieces, drained
½ cup shredded mozzarella cheese (2 ounces)

In a saucepan combine cream-style corn and flour. Add cream cheese and onion powder. Stir over low heat till cream cheese almost melts. Stir in whole kernel corn, mushrooms, and mozzarella cheese. Transfer to a 1½-quart casserole. Cover; chill 2 to 24 hours. Bake, covered, in a 400° oven for 50 minutes or till heated through.

Per serving: *194 cal., 7 g fat (4 g sat.), 21 mg chol., 7 g pro., 30 g carbo., 2 g dietary fiber, 494 mg sodium.*

A winter holiday doesn't go by at our house without this rich and creamy corn. I love it because it's so easy to make—my family loves it because it's so delicious to eat.

—Rosemary Hutchinson

BASIL CARROT-POTATO BAKE

Serves 4 or 5

2 cups shredded carrots (4 to 6 medium)
2 medium potatoes, peeled and cubed
½ cup plain yogurt *or* dairy sour cream
2 tablespoons margarine *or* butter
½ teaspoon dried basil, crushed
¼ teaspoon garlic salt *or* onion salt
⅛ teaspoon pepper

Cook the carrots and potatoes, covered, in a small amount of lightly salted boiling water for 15 to 20 minutes or till tender. Drain well. With an electric mixer on low speed or a potato masher, beat or mash the carrots and potatoes. Add the yogurt or sour cream, margarine or butter, basil, garlic salt or onion salt, and pepper. Beat mixture till smooth. Spoon 4 or 5 mounds on a greased 15x10x1-inch baking pan. Bake in a 500° oven for 10 to 12 minutes or till lightly browned.

Per serving: *152 cal., 6 g fat (1 g sat.), 2 mg chol., 3 g pro., 21 g carbo., 3 g dietary fiber, 216 mg sodium.*

Like most children, mine aren't crazy about cooked vegetables. So, I spruce up the flavor by mashing carrots and potatoes together, then I add yogurt or sour cream for richness.

—Sandra Granseth

SAVORY NEW POTATOES

Serves 4

1 medium onion, thinly sliced and separated into rings
2 tablespoons margarine *or* butter
1 pound whole tiny new potatoes, quartered
1 teaspoon ground coriander
⅛ teaspoon ground red pepper
Dash ground turmeric (optional)

In a medium saucepan cook the onion in hot margarine or butter till onion is tender but not brown, stirring occasionally. Add the potatoes, coriander, red pepper, and, if desired, turmeric. Cook, uncovered, over medium high heat till margarine or butter begins to bubble, stirring frequently. Reduce heat. Cook, covered, about 15 minutes more or till potatoes are tender, stirring occasionally.

Per serving: *177 cal., 6 g fat (1 g sat.), 0 mg chol., 3 g pro., 29 g carbo., 3 g dietary fiber, 77 mg sodium.*

Since the potatoes steam in their own juices, be sure to use a heavy saucepan with a tight-fitting lid to keep steam from escaping.

—Sharon Stilwell

MAKE-AHEAD MASHED POTATOES

With this dish, there's no last-minute hurry-scurry in the kitchen to get pipin' hot mashed potatoes on the table.

—Janet Figg

Serves 10

9 medium potatoes
1 8-ounce container sour cream dip with chives
1 3-ounce package cream cheese with chives, cut up
2 tablespoons margarine *or* butter
1 teaspoon onion salt
½ teaspoon garlic powder
¼ to ⅓ cup milk
1 tablespoon margarine *or* butter

Peel and quarter the potatoes. Cook, covered, in lightly salted boiling water for 20 to 25 minutes or till tender. Drain. With an electric mixer on low speed or with a potato masher, beat or mash the potatoes.

Add the sour cream dip, cream cheese, the 2 tablespoons margarine or butter, the onion salt, and garlic powder to the potatoes. Gradually beat in enough of the milk to make smooth and fluffy. Spoon the potato mixture into a greased 2-quart casserole. Cover and chill for up to 24 hours.

To serve, dot the potatoes with the remaining margarine or butter. Bake, uncovered, in a 325° oven for 60 to 65 minutes or till heated through.

Per serving: *187 cal., 8 g fat (4 g sat.), 11 mg chol., 3 g pro., 26 g carbo., 2 g dietary fiber, 222 mg sodium.*

POTATOES

PASTA E FAGIOLI (PASTA AND BEANS)

Serves 4 to 6

   2 cloves garlic, minced
   3 tablespoons olive oil
   2 10-ounce cans crushed tomatoes
   2 tablespoons capers, drained
   1 tablespoon honey
   1 tablespoon dried basil, crushed
   1 teaspoon dried rosemary, crushed
   1 teaspoon fennel seed
   1 teaspoon pepper
   ½ teaspoon crushed red pepper
   ¼ teaspoon salt
   1 pound penne, mostaccioli, *or* rigatoni
   1 15-ounce can garbanzo beans, drained
   1 cup freshly grated Parmesan cheese

   In a large saucepan cook the garlic in *2 tablespoons* of the olive oil till the garlic is golden, stirring constantly. Carefully add the remaining olive oil, tomatoes, capers, honey, basil, rosemary, fennel seed, pepper, crushed red pepper, and salt. Cook, uncovered, over medium-low heat for 20 to 25 minutes or till desired consistency, stirring occasionally.

   Meanwhile, cook the pasta according to package directions, adding the garbanzo beans the last 3 minutes of cooking. Drain well. Return the pasta and bean mixture to the hot saucepan. Add the tomato sauce. Gently toss to coat pasta. Transfer the pasta mixture to a warm serving bowl. Sprinkle with some of the Parmesan cheese. Pass the remaining cheese.

Per serving: *169 cal., 11 g fat (1 g sat.), 0 mg chol., 3 g pro., 19 g carbo., 3 g dietary fiber, 557 mg sodium.*

There are as many versions of this Italian dish as there are cooks, but my recipe adheres to the same principles as the rest of them— inexpensive, fast, and satisfying.

—Lisa Kingsley

CREAMY LEMON PASTA

*Grilled fresh yellowfin
tuna, Creamy Lemon
Pasta, and sourdough
bread—that's heaven!
And, easy too!*

—Diana McMillen

Serves 6

>   8 ounces fresh refrigerated *or* 6 ounces dried fettuccine
>   2 tablespoons unsalted butter, softened
>   2 teaspoons finely shredded lemon peel
>   1 cup whipping cream, warmed
>   ¾ cup freshly grated Parmesan cheese

Cook the pasta according to package directions. Drain well. Meanwhile, combine the softened butter and lemon peel; set aside.

Transfer the pasta to a warm serving bowl. Add the lemon butter and warm whipping cream. Toss gently to coat pasta. Sprinkle some of the Parmesan cheese over the top. Pass the remaining Parmesan cheese.

Per serving: *357 cal., 22 g fat (14 g sat.), 81 mg chol., 10 g pro., 30 g carbo., 1 g dietary fiber, 204 mg sodium.*

LIGHT AND LEMONY FETTUCCINE

*I love to turn plain
pasta into a something-
special dish. A
sprinkling of lemon peel
and a little pepper does
just that!*
—Sharon Stilwell

Serves 6

>   6 ounces fresh refrigerated fettuccine
>   6 ounces fresh refrigerated spinach fettuccine
>   1 tablespoon margarine *or* butter
>   ½ teaspoon finely shredded lemon peel
>   ¼ teaspoon pepper

Cook pasta according to package directions. Drain well. Return the pasta to the hot saucepan. Add the margarine or butter, lemon peel, and pepper. Toss gently to coat pasta.

Per serving: *175 cal., 3 g fat (1 g sat.), 5 mg chol., 6 g pro., 32 g carbo., 2 g dietary fiber, 30 mg sodium.*

CARAMELIZED ONIONS AND RICE

Serves 4 or 5

1 medium onion, cut into thin wedges
1 teaspoon sugar
2 tablespoons margarine *or* butter
2 cups chicken broth
1 cup long grain rice
1 10-ounce package frozen chopped spinach, thawed and well drained

In a medium saucepan cook the onion and sugar in hot margarine or butter over medium-high heat till onion is golden brown, stirring constantly. Carefully add the chicken broth and rice. Bring mixture to boiling; reduce heat. Cover and simmer about 15 minutes or till rice is tender and liquid is absorbed. Stir in the spinach, then heat through.

Per serving: *268 cal., 7 g fat (1 g sat.), 1 mg chol., 8 g pro., 44 g carbo., 3 g dietary fiber, 518 mg sodium.*

Several years ago, a similar recipe appeared in a magazine. Through the many times of making it, I have converted a somewhat time-consuming recipe into an easy, pilaf-type dish with the same terrific onion flavor.

—Sharon Stilwell

CURRY AND APRICOT PILAF

Serves 6

1 cup long grain rice
⅓ cup snipped dried apricots
¼ cup light raisins
1 tablespoon dried minced onion
1 tablespoon instant chicken bouillon granules
1 teaspoon sugar
1 teaspoon curry powder
2 cups water
1 tablespoon margarine *or* butter

In a 1-quart saucepan stir together the rice, apricots, raisins, onion, chicken bouillon granules, sugar, and curry powder. Stir in the water and margarine or butter. Bring mixture to boiling; reduce heat. Cover and simmer about 15 minutes or till rice is tender and liquid is absorbed. Fluff with a fork before serving.

Per serving: *177 cal., 2 g fat (0 g sat.), 0 mg chol., 3 g pro., 36 g carbo., 2 g dietary fiber, 476 mg sodium.*

For convenience sake, make the dry pilaf mix ahead and keep it on hand for a quick side dish. Simply measure one recipe of the dry ingredients into each plastic bag and seal. To cook the mix, add the water and margarine.

—Nancy Byal

For brunch, enjoy dainty Dried Cherry Tea Cakes (page 88) and Grandma's Danish Rolls (page 101).

BREADS TO BRAG ABOUT

Blueberry-bustin' muffins, crusty Italian sourdough, dainty heart-shaped tea cakes—the basketful of goodies on the following pages stir up touching memories of our grandmothers' and mothers' kitchens, where many of us learned to bake. We hope the bread recipes that are so dear to us become new favorites in your kitchen. Better yet, maybe you'll pass them down to those you love.

DRIED-CHERRY TEA CAKES

Serves 20 to 24

¼ cup **cherry juice** *or* **orange juice**
1 3-ounce package **dried cherries,** chopped (¾ cup)
3 cups **all-purpose flour**
1½ teaspoons **baking powder**
½ teaspoon **salt**
2¼ cups **sugar**
1 cup **cooking oil**
3 **eggs**
1½ cups **milk**
1 tablespoon **poppy seed**
2 teaspoons **almond extract**
1½ teaspoons **vanilla**
1 recipe **Cherry Glaze**

In a small saucepan bring cherry or orange juice to boiling. Remove from heat; add cherries. Let stand for 5 minutes. Drain, squeezing juice from cherries. Reserve cherries and juice.

Grease 4-inch heart-shaped tins or regular muffin cups. In a small mixing bowl stir together flour, baking powder, and salt. Set aside.

In a large mixing bowl combine sugar, oil, and eggs. Beat with an electric mixer on low speed till combined. Alternately add flour mixture and milk, beating on low to medium speed just till combined. Add drained cherries, poppy seed, almond extract, and vanilla; beat till combined.

Pour batter into prepared heart-shaped tins or muffin cups. Bake in a 350° oven for 15 to 20 minutes or till a wooden toothpick inserted near the center of the cakes comes out clean. Place a wire rack over waxed paper. Remove cakes from pans; place on rack. Brush tops and sides of warm cakes with Cherry Glaze. Cool about 30 minutes or till glaze no longer is sticky.

Cherry Glaze: In a small saucepan combine ¾ cup *sugar* and ¼ cup *cherry* or *orange juice.* Bring to boiling, stirring constantly. Cook and stir till sugar is dissolved. Remove from heat. If desired, stir in 1 tablespoon *cherry* or *raspberry liqueur.*

Per serving: *320 cal., 12 g fat (2 g sat. fat), 34 mg chol., 4 g pro., 49 g carbo., 1 g dietary fiber, 201 mg sodium.*

AMISH BREAKFAST PUFFS WITH DRIED CHERRIES

Serves 12

1½ cups all-purpose flour
½ cup sugar
1½ teaspoons baking powder
½ teaspoon salt
¼ teaspoon ground mace
1 egg
½ cup milk
⅓ cup cooking oil
1 teaspoon vanilla
¾ cup dried cherries *or* raisins
½ cup sugar
1 teaspoon ground cinnamon
6 tablespoons margarine *or* butter, melted

Grease 12 regular muffin cups or line them with paper bake cups. Set aside.

In a medium mixing bowl stir together flour, the first ½ cup sugar, the baking powder, salt, and mace. Make a well in the center of the dry mixture.

In small mixing bowl beat the egg slightly with a fork. Stir in milk, cooking oil, and vanilla. Add the egg mixture all at once to the dry mixture. Stir just till moistened (batter should be lumpy). Fold in cherries or raisins.

Spoon batter into the prepared muffin cups, filling each ⅔ full. Bake in a 350° oven for 15 to 20 minutes or till the tops of the muffins are firm and golden.

Meanwhile, in a small shallow bowl stir together the remaining ½ cup sugar and the cinnamon. Remove muffins from cups while hot; roll tops in melted margarine or butter, then in cinnamon-sugar mixture. Serve warm.

Per serving: *265 cal., 13 g fat (5 g sat. fat), 34 mg chol., 3 g pro., 36 g carbo., 1 g dietary fiber, 184 mg sodium.*

Lightly spiced, warm and tender, with a buttery sugar topping— good reasons why this recipe earns five stars at our house.

—Diana McMillen

BIG BLUEBERRY MUFFINS

For muffins you can barely get your fingers around, fill the muffin cups completely full and bake at a slightly higher temperature than for regular-size muffins.

—Diane Yanney

Serves 6

1⅓ cups all-purpose flour
¼ cup sugar
2 teaspoons baking powder
½ teaspoon salt
1 egg
½ cup milk
¼ cup cooking oil
½ teaspoon vanilla
½ cup fresh *or* frozen blueberries

Grease 6 regular muffin cups and the entire top of the pan. Set muffin cups aside.

In a medium mixing bowl stir together flour, sugar, baking powder, and salt. Make a well in the center of the dry mixture.

In small mixing bowl slightly beat the egg with a fork. Stir in milk, cooking oil, and vanilla. Add egg mixture all at once to the dry mixture. Stir just till moistened (batter should be lumpy). Fold in blueberries.

Spoon batter into the prepared muffin cups, filling each ⅔ full. Bake in a 425° oven for 15 to 20 minutes or till tops of muffins are firm and golden. Remove muffins from muffin cups and cool slightly on a wire rack. Serve warm.

Per serving: *244 cal., 11 g fat (2 g sat. fat), 37 mg chol., 5 g pro., 33 g carbo., 1 g dietary fiber, 296 mg sodium.*

SPICED APPLE MUFFIN CAKE

Serves 12

    2 cups all-purpose flour
 1¼ cups sugar
    1 tablespoon baking powder
 1½ teaspoons apple pie spice
    ½ teaspoon baking soda
    ½ teaspoon salt
    2 eggs
    1 8-ounce carton dairy sour cream
    ¼ cup margarine *or* butter, melted
    1 cup peeled, shredded apple
    3 tablespoons sugar
    2 tablespoons all-purpose flour
    ¼ teaspoon apple pie spice
    4 teaspoons margarine *or* butter

Grease and lightly flour a 7- to 8-cup soufflé dish or an 8-inch springform pan. Set aside.

In a large mixing bowl stir together the 2 cups flour, 1¼ cups sugar, the baking powder, the 1½ teaspoons apple pie spice, the baking soda, and salt. Make a well in the center of the dry mixture.

In a medium mixing bowl slightly beat eggs with a fork. Stir in sour cream and melted margarine or butter. Add egg mixture all at once to the dry mixture. Stir just till moistened (batter should be lumpy). Fold in shredded apple. Spread batter in the prepared pan or dish.

For topping, in a small mixing bowl combine the remaining sugar, flour, and spice. Cut in the remaining margarine or butter till the mixture resembles coarse crumbs. Sprinkle topping atop batter in pan.

Bake in a 350° oven about 1 hour or till a wooden pick inserted near the center comes out clean. Cool in the dish on a wire rack for 20 minutes. Remove cake from dish and cool on the rack. Serve warm or cool.

Per serving: *279 cal., 10 g fat (4 g sat. fat), 44 mg chol., 4 g pro., 44 g carbo., 1 g dietary fiber, 277 mg sodium.*

Baking this coffee cake in a soufflé dish makes it look like a giant muffin. You'll love the spicy fruit flavor and generous streusel topping.

—Nancy Byal

SPANISH COFFEE CAKE

Serves 18

2½ **cups all-purpose flour**
 1 **cup packed brown sugar**
 ¾ **cup sugar**
 1 **teaspoon ground cinnamon**
 ½ **teaspoon salt**
 ¾ **cup cooking oil**
 1 **teaspoon baking soda**
 1 **teaspoon baking powder**
 1 **cup buttermilk**
 1 **beaten egg**

Grease and flour a 13x9x2-inch baking pan. Set aside.

In a medium mixing bowl stir together flour, brown sugar, sugar, cinnamon, and salt. Make a well in the center of the mixture. Add cooking oil; stir to mix. Remove *1 cup* of the flour-oil mixture for topping; set aside.

To the remaining flour-oil mixture, stir in baking soda and baking powder. Add buttermilk and egg; stir just till moistened.

Spread batter in the prepared baking pan. Sprinkle with the reserved topping. Bake in a 350° oven for 35 to 40 minutes or till a wooden pick inserted near the center comes out clean. Cool in the pan on a wire rack.

Per serving: *231 cal., 10 g fat (1 g sat. fat), 12 mg chol., 3 g pro., 34 g carbo., 1 g dietary fiber, 145 mg sodium.*

QUICK-AND-EASY COFFEE CAKE

Serves 6

1 cup all-purpose flour
½ cup sugar
1 tablespoon baking powder
⅛ teaspoon salt
½ cup milk
¼ cup cooking oil
1 egg
2 tablespoons sugar
½ teaspoon ground cinnamon

Grease an 8x8x2-inch baking pan and set it aside. In a medium mixing bowl stir together flour, the ½ cup sugar, the baking powder, and salt. Make a well in the center of the dry mixture.

In a small mixing bowl stir together milk, oil, and egg. (I use a glass measure for this step. First, add milk to the ½-cup line. Then, carefully pour in oil till liquid level is at ¾-cup line. Add the egg and beat with a fork to combine.)

Add the egg mixture all at once to the dry mixture. Stir just till moistened (batter should be lumpy). Pour the batter into the prepared baking pan. For the topping, stir together the 2 tablespoons sugar and the cinnamon; sprinkle evenly over batter.

Bake in a 375° oven for 12 to 15 minutes or till wooden pick inserted near the center comes out clean. Cool slightly in the pan on a wire rack. Serve warm.

Per serving: *262 cal., 11 g fat (2 g sat. fat), 37 mg chol., 4 g pro., 38 g carbo., 1 g dietary fiber, 211 mg sodium.*

This stir-together recipe came from the Kitchen-Klatter folks of Shenandoah, Iowa. For years, they had a daily radio program and distributed a small monthly magazine in our area. My mother showed me how to make this simple snack cake, and now I've taught my own daughter.

—Sharyl Heiken

SOUR CREAM COFFEE CAKE

Every fall, my family would gather black walnuts in the woods on our farm. I became so accustomed to the distinct flavor of black walnuts that I prefer them to English walnuts in this coffee cake.

—Marilyn Cornelius

Serves 12 to 16

- 2 **cups all-purpose flour**
- 1 **teaspoon baking powder**
- 1 **teaspoon baking soda**
- ½ **cup margarine** *or* **butter**
- 1 **cup sugar**
- 1 **teaspoon vanilla**
- 3 **eggs**
- 1 **8-ounce carton dairy sour cream**
- ¾ **cup packed brown sugar**
- ½ **cup sugar**
- ¾ **cup chopped black walnuts** *or* **other nuts**
- ½ **teaspoon ground cinnamon**

Grease a 13x9x2-inch baking pan. In a mixing bowl stir together flour, baking powder, and baking soda. Set pan and flour mixture aside.

In large mixing bowl beat margarine or butter with an electric mixer on medium to high speed about 30 seconds or till softened. Add the 1 cup sugar and the vanilla to margarine and beat till fluffy. Add eggs, one at a time, beating on medium speed till combined. Alternately add flour mixture and sour cream to egg mixture, beating on low to medium speed after each addition just till combined.

For filling, in small mixing bowl stir together brown sugar, ½ cup sugar, the nuts, and cinnamon. Spread *half* the batter in the prepared baking pan; sprinkle *half* of the nut filling atop. Repeat layers. Bake in a 350° oven about 50 minutes or till a wooden pick inserted near the center comes out clean. Cool slightly in the pan on a wire rack. Serve warm.

Per serving: *399 cal., 17 g fat (5 g sat. fat), 62 mg chol., 6 g pro., 56 g carbo., 1 g dietary fiber, 214 mg sodium.*

BLUEBERRY BREAD

Serves 32

1½ cups fresh *or* frozen blueberries
2½ cups all-purpose flour
  1 teaspoon baking soda
  ¼ teaspoon salt
  1 cup packed light brown sugar
  ½ cup sugar
  ⅔ cup cooking oil
  1 egg
  1 teaspoon vanilla
  1 cup sour milk
  ½ cup chopped pecans
  ½ cup sugar
  1 tablespoon margarine *or* butter, melted

Grease two 8x4x2-inch loaf pans. Rinse and drain blueberries. In a small mixing bowl stir together flour, baking soda, and salt. Set pans, blueberries, and the flour mixture aside.

In a large mixing bowl combine brown sugar, the first ½ cup sugar, the oil, egg, and vanilla. Beat with an electric mixer on medium speed for 1 to 2 minutes or till combined. Alternately add flour mixture and sour milk, beating on low to medium speed after each addition just till combined. Gently stir in blueberries and pecans.

For topping, combine remaining ½ cup sugar and melted margarine or butter and stir till crumbly. Pour batter into prepared loaf pans. Sprinkle sugar mixture atop. Bake in a 350° oven for 40 to 45 minutes or till a wooden pick inserted near the center comes out clean. Cool loaves in the pans on a wire rack for 10 minutes. Remove from pans and completely cool on the rack.

Per serving: *151 cal., 7 g fat (1 g sat. fat), 7 mg chol., 2 g pro., 22 g carbo., 1 g dietary fiber, 56 mg sodium.*

Living along the shores of Lake Michigan, my family picked wild blueberries and ate them in just about anything. Today, even though Iowa is now our home, my children and I still love blueberries as much as ever.

—Patty Beebout

OLD-FASHIONED BANANA BREAD

When a friend and I were about 10, we baked this recipe for a 4-H Club demonstration. We spent our summer making it three or four times a week, and our once-enthusiastic families grew pretty tired of it. Now, more than 20 years later, the bread is a top request once again. And, my friend is married to my brother!

—Marilyn Cornelius

Serves 18

  2 **cups all-purpose flour**
1½ **teaspoons baking powder**
  ½ **teaspoon baking soda**
  ½ **cup margarine** *or* **butter**
  1 **cup sugar**
  2 **eggs**
  1 **cup mashed bananas (2** *or* **3 medium)**
  2 **tablespoons milk**
  1 **teaspoon lemon juice**

Grease one 9x5x3-inch loaf pan or three 4½x2½x1½-inch loaf pans. In a small mixing bowl stir together flour, baking powder, and baking soda. Set pan(s) and flour mixture aside.

In large mixing bowl beat margarine or butter with an electric mixer on medium to high speed about 30 seconds or till softened. Add sugar and beat till fluffy. Then add eggs, one at a time, beating on medium speed till combined. Add bananas, milk, and lemon juice; beat till combined. Add flour mixture; beat on low to medium speed just till combined.

Pour batter into prepared pan(s). Bake in a 350° oven about 45 minutes or till a wooden pick inserted near the center comes out clean. Cool loaf in the pan on a wire rack for 10 minutes. Remove from the pan(s); completely cool on the rack. Wrap and store at room temperature overnight before slicing.

Per serving: *160 cal., 6 g fat (1 g sat. fat), 24 mg chol., 2 g pro., 25 g carbo., 1 g dietary fiber, 114 mg sodium.*

BANANA BREAD FRENCH TOAST

Serves 4

  2 **eggs**
¼ **cup milk**
½ **teaspoon vanilla**
¼ **teaspoon ground cinnamon**
⅛ **teaspoon ground nutmeg**
½ **loaf leftover banana bread, cut into ½-inch-thick slices (about 8 slices)**
Margarine *or* butter
Maple syrup *or* powdered sugar

In a shallow bowl beat eggs. Stir in milk, vanilla, cinnamon, and nutmeg. Gently dip sliced banana bread into egg mixture, coating both sides.

In a nonstick skillet or on a griddle cook bread in a small amount of hot margarine or butter over medium heat for 2 to 3 minutes on each side or till golden brown, adding more margarine as needed. Serve with maple syrup or powdered sugar.

Per serving: *443 cal., 14 g fat (3 g sat. fat), 55 mg chol., 5 g pro., 77 g carbo., 1 g dietary fiber, 218 mg sodium.*

There's no such thing as leftover bananas in our house because we often bake banana bread. What do we do with leftover banana bread? Use it to make French toast for a delicious breakfast treat.

—Kristi Fuller

NORWEGIAN CHRISTMAS BREAD

Serves 24

4¾ to 5¼ cups all-purpose flour
2 packages active dry yeast
¾ teaspoon ground cardamom
1¼ cups milk
½ cup sugar
½ cup butter *or* margarine
½ teaspoon salt
1 egg
1 cup currants *or* raisins
½ cup candied red *or* green cherries
½ cup diced candied citron *or* mixed candied fruits and peels
1 egg
1 tablespoon water
2 tablespoons butter *or* margarine, melted
2 tablespoons sugar
½ teaspoon ground cinnamon

In a large mixing bowl stir together *2 cups* of the flour, the yeast, and cardamom. In a medium saucepan combine milk, ½ cup sugar, the ½ cup butter or margarine, and the salt; heat and stir just till warm (120° to 130°) and butter is almost melted. Add milk mixture to flour mixture; add an egg. Beat with an electric mixer on low speed for 30 seconds, scraping the sides of the bowl constantly. Beat on high speed for 3 minutes. Using a wooden spoon, stir in currants or raisins, cherries, citron or mixed fruits, and as much of the remaining flour as you can.

Turn dough out onto a lightly floured surface. Knead in enough of the remaining flour to make a moderately stiff dough that is smooth and elastic (6 to 8 minutes total). Shape the dough into a ball. Place in a lightly greased bowl; turn once to grease surface. Cover and let rise in a warm place till double (about 1½ hours).

Punch dough down. Turn out onto a lightly floured surface. Divide in half. Cover; let rest for 10 minutes. Shape into 2 round loaves; place on greased baking sheets. Slightly flatten each to a 6-inch diameter. Cover and let rise in a warm place till almost double (45 to 60 minutes).

In a small bowl beat egg and water; brush onto loaves. Bake in a 375° oven for 30 to 35 minutes or till the tops are golden and loaves sound hollow when tapped. If necessary, cover loosely with foil the last 10 to 15 minutes to prevent overbrowning.

Brush the loaves with melted butter or margarine. In a small bowl combine the 2 tablespoons sugar and cinnamon; sprinkle over loaves. Transfer to a wire rack to cool.

Per serving: *209 cal., 6 g fat (3 g sat. fat), 32 mg chol., 4 g pro., 36 g carbo., 1 g dietary fiber, 111 mg sodium.*

This cardamom-scented fruit bread makes two loaves, so you can freeze one for later or give it away.

When my grandmother emigrated from Norway, she brought part of her homeland with her—in her recipe box. Every Christmas, she'd bake this bread, Julekage, *and we'd eat it with thinly sliced* gjetost *(goat cheese) or* rollepolse *(a spiced cured meat).*

—Julia Malloy

SICILIAN SOURDOUGH COUNTRY BREAD

This bread reminds me of my great grandmother's childhood home in Sicily. There, my relatives bake discus-size loaves of bread in the large brick oven at their campagna, *or "country place." The sourdough makes the bread extra chewy, and semolina flour adds extra crunch.*

—Lisa Kingsley

Serves 24

> 4 to 4½ cups all-purpose flour
> 1½ cups warm water (120° to 130°)
> 1 cup semolina flour
> 1 cup Sourdough Starter
> 2 tablespoons honey
> 2 teaspoons salt
> ½ teaspoon baking soda
> **Cornmeal**

In a large nonmetal mixing bowl stir together *2 cups* of the all-purpose flour, the water, semolina flour, Sourdough Starter, and honey. Cover with clear plastic wrap or a damp towel; let stand in a warm place overnight.

In a small mixing bowl stir together *1 cup* of the all-purpose flour, the salt, and baking soda. Stir flour mixture into starter mixture; beat with an electric mixer on medium speed till smooth. Using a wooden spoon, stir in as much of the remaining flour as you can.

Turn dough out onto a lightly floured surface. Knead in enough of the remaining flour to make a moderately stiff dough that is smooth and elastic (about 8 minutes).

Lightly grease a baking sheet; sprinkle with cornmeal. Shape the dough into one large or two small round loaves. Place on a baking sheet. Cover with a damp towel; let rise in a warm place till double (about 2 hours).

Use a serrated knife to slash the tops of the loaves diagonally about ½ inch deep. Place in a 425° oven. (For a crisp crust, spray the loaves with cold water every 3 minutes for the first 10 minutes of baking.) After 10 minutes, reduce the heat to 375°; bake about 20 minutes more or till the bread sounds hollow when you tap the top with your finger. (If necessary, cover loosely with foil the last 15 minutes of baking to prevent overbrowning.) Immediately remove bread from pans. Cool on wire racks.

Sourdough Starter: In a nonmetal mixing bowl combine 2 cups *all-purpose flour,* 2 cups warm *water* (105° to 115°), 1 tablespoon *active dry yeast,* and 1 tablespoon *sugar.* Cover with cheesecloth and let stand in a warm place for 48 hours. Store in the refrigerator.

To use, stir starter and measure amount called for in recipe. To replenish starter, stir in 1 cup *all-purpose flour* and 1 cup *warm water* (120° to 130°); let stand in a warm place for a few hours until bubbles appear again. Return to the refrigerator. If starter goes unused for 2 weeks, remove 1 cup starter and replenish.

Per serving: *127 cal., 0 g fat (0 g sat. fat), 0 mg chol., 4 g pro., 27 g carbo., 1 g dietary fiber, 196 mg sodium.*

GRANDMA'S DANISH ROLLS

Serves 24

> 2 packages active dry yeast
> 1⅓ cups margarine *or* butter, softened
> 1 cup milk
> ¼ cup sugar
> 4½ to 5 cups all-purpose flour
> 2 beaten eggs
> 1½ cups sifted powdered sugar
> 1 cup ground nuts
> ⅛ teaspoon salt
> ½ teaspoon almond extract

Soften yeast in ¼ cup *warm water* (105° to 115°) for 5 minutes. In a saucepan combine *½ cup* of the margarine, the milk, sugar, and 1 teaspoon *salt*. Heat and stir just till warm (120° to 130°) and margarine is almost melted. Turn into a large bowl. Stir in *2 cups* of the flour; beat with an electric mixer for 30 seconds, scraping bowl constantly. Add yeast mixture and eggs; beat for 3 minutes. Stir in as much of the remaining flour as you can.

On a lightly floured surface knead in enough remaining flour to make a moderately stiff dough that is smooth and elastic (6 to 8 minutes). Shape into a ball. Put in a lightly greased bowl; turn. Cover; let rise in a warm place till double (about 1 hour).

For filling, combine ⅓ cup of the margarine and *1 cup* of the powdered sugar. Stir in nuts, salt, and *¼ teaspoon* of the almond extract.

Punch dough down; turn out onto a lightly floured surface. Cover; let rest for 10 minutes. Roll dough into a 21x10-inch rectangle. Brush with *¼ cup* of the margarine. Fold dough crosswise into thirds, forming a 10x7-inch rectangle; press edges to seal. (Chill for 20 minutes if dough starts to get too soft.) Roll dough again into a 21x10-inch rectangle; spread with remaining ¼ cup margarine. Fold into thirds, forming a 10x7-inch rectangle; press edges to seal. Chill, if necessary.

Roll dough into a 22x12-inch rectangle. Spread filling lengthwise over half the dough. Fold dough in half lengthwise, forming a 22x6-inch rectangle; press edges to seal. Cut rectangle crosswise into twenty-four strips. Twist each strip 4 or 5 times. Place strips 4 inches apart on a lightly greased baking sheet. Form each into a snail shape, tucking ends underneath. Cover; let rise in a warm place till nearly double (45 to 60 minutes). Bake in a 350° oven for 15 to 18 minutes or till golden.

For frosting, stir together remaining ½ cup powdered sugar and remaining ¼ teaspoon almond extract. Add enough *hot water* (2 to 3 teaspoons) to make an icing of drizzling consistency. Frost rolls while warm.

Per serving: *253 cal., 14 g fat (4 g sat. fat), 26 mg chol., 4 g pro., 28 g carbo., 1 g dietary fiber, 222 mg sodium.*

My Danish grandmother passed the recipe for these rich rolls along to me. My first experiences baking them were for a 4-H cooking competition and as an entry in the Iowa State Fair.

—Heidi McNutt

JONNYCAKES

Serves 4

    1 cup cornmeal
    1 tablespoon sugar
    1 teaspoon salt
  1⅓ cups hot water
    ⅔ cup milk
    2 tablespoons margarine *or* butter
Maple syrup

In a medium mixing bowl stir together cornmeal, sugar, and salt. Add hot water; stir till smooth. Cover and let stand in a warm place for 5 minutes.

Meanwhile, in a 2-cup microwave-safe measure combine milk and margarine or butter. Micro-cook, uncovered, on 100% power (high) for 1½ to 2 minutes or till margarine is melted. Add milk mixture to cornmeal mixture; stir till smooth.

Drop batter by tablespoons onto a hot, lightly greased skillet. Cook till pancakes have bubbly surfaces and slightly dry edges; turn and cook second sides till pancakes are golden. Serve immediately with maple syrup.

Per pancake with 1 teaspoon syrup: *71 cal., 3 g fat (1 g sat. fat), 4 mg chol., 1 g pro., 11 g carbo., 1 g dietary fiber, 121 mg sodium.*

A true Rhode Islander would use only white cornmeal that's grown and stone-ground in the state, but I've used all grinds and colors of cornmeal with success. The variable is the amount of liquid needed, give or take a tablespoon. The consistency of the batter should be that of a thick pancake batter. Regardless of the cornmeal you use, always serve these silver-dollar-size hotcakes with maple syrup.

—Jan Hazard

PINEAPPLE BRUNCH BAGELS

Serves 16 to 20

> 1 8-ounce container soft-style cream cheese with pineapple
> 8 to 10 frozen miniature bagels, thawed, split, and toasted
> ⅓ cup coconut, toasted
> 16 to 20 whole almonds, toasted

Place cream cheese in a pastry bag fitted with a medium-size star tip. Pipe about *1 tablespoon* of the cream cheese atop *each* bagel half. Top *each* bagel half with toasted coconut and an almond. Serve immediately or cover and chill for up to 1 hour.

Per serving: *101 cal., 5 g fat (3 g sat. fat), 13 mg chol., 2 g pro., 11 g carbo., 1 g dietary fiber, 116 mg sodium.*

Cream cheese piped through a pastry bag and decorating tip dresses up ordinary mini bagels, but go ahead and spread it on, if you're in a hurry. For a splash of red, substitute fresh strawberries for the almonds when they're in season.

—Shelli McConnell

TOASTED PARMESAN BREAD

Serves 3 or 4

> ¼ cup grated Parmesan cheese
> ¼ cup mayonnaise *or* salad dressing
> 6 to 8 slices French bread

In a small mixing bowl stir together Parmesan cheese and mayonnaise or salad dressing. Spread onto one side of French bread slices. Arrange slices, cheese side up, on the unheated rack of a broiler pan. Broil about 5 inches from heat for 3 to 4 minutes or till golden and bubbly. Serve warm.

Per serving: *229 cal., 18 g fat (4 g sat. fat), 16 mg chol., 5 g pro., 13 g carbo., 0 g dietary fiber, 365 mg sodium.*

These cheesy treats taste delicious as appetizers or as accompaniments to soups and salads. Turn to page 66 to see them pictured with Greens with Honey-Mustard Dressing.

—Kay Cargill

Billowy whipped cream tops off Vanilla-Cinnamon Cream Pie (page 106).

BEST-LOVED DESSERTS

A "best-loved" dessert means more than just a tasty recipe. It's a recipe we turn to time and time again because we know that every forkful will satisfy our loved ones. We offer the desserts in this section, some dazzlingly decadent and others down-home delicious, in hopes they will find a warm place in your heart, as they have in ours.

VANILLA-CINNAMON CREAM PIE

Serves 8

   1 **medium orange**
   3 **cups milk**
   6 **inches stick cinnamon, broken up**
  ⅔ **cup sugar**
  ¼ **cup cornstarch**
   2 **beaten eggs**
   1 **tablespoon margarine *or* butter**
1½ **teaspoons vanilla**
  ¼ **cup apricot preserves**
   1 **recipe Pastry for Single-Crust Pie**
  ½ **cup whipping cream**
   1 **tablespoon orange liqueur *or* powdered sugar**

With a vegetable peeler, cut peel from orange in strips. Cut peel into thin strips. In a heavy saucepan combine orange peel strips, milk, and stick cinnamon. Cook and stir mixture over low heat 15 minutes. Remove from heat; cool slightly. Strain milk into a medium bowl; discard peel and stick cinnamon. In same saucepan combine sugar and cornstarch. Gradually stir in warm milk. Cook and stir over medium-high heat till mixture is thickened and bubbly. Reduce heat; cook and stir 2 minutes more. Remove from heat. Gradually stir *1 cup* hot mixture into beaten eggs. Return all of the egg mixture to the saucepan. Bring to a gentle boil (do not boil rapidly). Cook and stir 2 minutes more. Remove from heat. Stir in margarine or butter and vanilla.

In a small saucepan heat preserves till melted; spoon onto bottom of baked pastry shell. Gently pour hot filling atop preserves. Cover the surface with plastic wrap. Chill. In a small mixer bowl beat whipping cream and liqueur or powdered sugar with an electric mixer on low speed till soft peaks form. Drop from a spoon into mounds atop pie. Sprinkle with *ground cinnamon,* if desired. Cover; chill till serving.

Pastry for Single-Crust Pie: In a mixing bowl stir together 1¼ cups *all-purpose flour* and ¼ teaspoon *salt.* Cut in ⅓ cup *shortening* till pieces are size of small peas. Sprinkle 1 tablespoon *cold water* over part of mixture; toss with a fork. Push to side of bowl. Repeat with more water (2 to 3 tablespoons) till all is moistened. Form dough into a ball. On a lightly floured surface, flatten dough with hands. Roll dough from center to edges, forming a 12-inch circle. Wrap pastry around rolling pin. Unroll onto a 9-inch pie plate. Ease pastry into pie plate, being careful not to stretch pastry. Trim pastry to ½ inch beyond edge of pie plate; fold under extra pastry. With a fork, prick bottom and sides of pastry. Bake in a 450° oven 10 to 12 minutes or till golden. Cool.

Per serving: *391 cal., 19 g fat (7 g sat. fat), 82 mg chol., 7 g pro., 49 g carbo., 1 g dietary fiber, 152 mg sodium.*

HARVEST APPLE TART

Serves 12 to 16

    2 oranges
    ⅓ cup Madeira *or* cream sherry
    ¼ cup sugar
    3 inches stick cinnamon
    2 whole cloves
    3 medium apples, peeled, cored, and halved lengthwise
    2 teaspoons cornstarch
    1 recipe Harvest Pastry Shell
    ½ cup seedless red *or* green grapes, halved

Cut a 2x1-inch section of peel from 1 orange; reserve peel. Juice the oranges (need ½ cup). In a saucepan combine reserved peel, orange juice, Madeira or sherry, sugar, cinnamon, cloves, and ⅓ cup *water.* Add apple halves. Bring to boiling; reduce heat. Cover; simmer 15 to 18 minutes or just till tender, turning once. Remove apples, reserving liquid. Cool apples. To fan each apple half, make 7 to 10 lengthwise cuts from one end to, but not through, opposite end. For glaze, remove spices and peel from reserved liquid. Measure *¾ cup* reserved liquid and return to pan; discard any remaining liquid. Combine cornstarch and 1 tablespoon *cold water;* stir into reserved liquid. Cook and stir till thickened and bubbly. Cook and stir 2 minutes more. Remove from heat; cool slightly. Arrange fanned apples on the baked Harvest Pastry Shell. Sprinkle grapes into spaces between apples. Spoon glaze over fruit. Chill at least 2 hours.

Harvest Pastry Shell: In a mixing bowl combine 2 cups *all-purpose flour,* 3 table-spoons *sugar,* and ¼ teaspoon *salt.* With a pastry blender, cut in ¾ cup *margarine* or *butter* till pieces are size of fine crumbs. Combine 1 beaten *egg yolk* and ¼ cup *cold water;* gradually add to flour mixture, mixing well. Knead lightly to form a ball. Cover; chill 1 hour or till easy to handle. On a lightly floured surface roll *two-thirds* of the dough into a 13-inch circle. Trim, if necessary. Transfer to a baking sheet. Fold dough under, about ¾ inch, around the edge to make a smooth, flat rim. Roll remaining pastry to ⅛-inch thickness. With a small knife or leaf-shaped cutter, cut dough into 30 to 36 grape-leaf shapes, each about 1½ inches long. Score veins in leaves with back of a knife. Use scraps to make ¼-inch balls. Brush rim of dough circle with water. Arrange balls in clusters, like grapes, on the rim; fill in with leaves. Combine 1 *egg yolk* and 1 teaspoon *water;* divide among 3 small bowls. Mix in *food coloring* to make shades of gold, green, and purple. Using a small brush, paint leaves and grapes. Prick bottom of crust; brush bottom with water and sprinkle with 1 tablespoon *sugar.* Bake in a 450° oven 6 to 7 minutes or till light brown. Cool. Transfer to a large, flat platter.

Per serving: *252 cal., 12 g fat (2 g sat. fat), 18 mg chol., 3 g pro., 33 g carbo., 2 g dietary fiber, 180 mg sodium.*

As a food stylist, I enjoy making food look as good as it tastes. For this autumn tart, I use a glaze made with food coloring to paint the pastry grapes purple and the leaves green and gold.

—Janet Herwig

APPLE CRUMB PIE

One of my high school teachers gave me this easy-to-make pie recipe. In all the years I've made the pie, it has never failed. Maybe it's because the crumb crust is much simpler than a regular pastry crust. For an extra-special treat, top each pie wedge with a scoop of cinnamon ice cream.

—Heidi McNutt

Serves 8

1½ **cups all-purpose flour**
1½ **teaspoons sugar**
  1 **teaspoon salt**
  ⅓ **cup cooking oil**
  2 **tablespoons skim milk**
  ¾ **cup all-purpose flour**
  ½ **cup sugar**
  ⅓ **cup margarine *or* butter**
  ½ **cup sugar**
  1 **teaspoon ground cinnamon**
  6 **to 8 large baking apples (such as Granny Smith), peeled, cored, and cut into ½-inch slices**

For crust, in a 9-inch pie plate stir together the 1½ cups flour, the 1½ teaspoons sugar, and the salt. Form a well in the center. With a fork, beat together cooking oil and milk. Pour into dry ingredients. With a wooden spoon, stir mixture till it forms a ball. With fingers or back of a spoon, pat mixture into pie pan to form a crust. Chill till needed.

For crumb topping, in a small mixing bowl combine the ¾ cup flour and the first ½ cup sugar. With a pastry blender or 2 forks, cut in the margarine or butter till mixture is the size of peas.

In a small bowl combine the remaining ½ cup sugar and cinnamon. Sprinkle *half* of the cinnamon mixture over bottom of pie crust. Add apples to crust. Sprinkle with remaining cinnamon mixture. Sprinkle with crumb topping, patting slightly into apple mixture. Bake in a 425° oven for 10 minutes; reduce temperature to 350° and continue baking for 50 to 60 minutes or till bubbly around the edges. If needed, cover edges with foil during the last 30 minutes of baking to prevent overbrowning. Serve warm.

Per serving: *436 cal., 17 g fat (3 g sat. fat), 0 mg chol., 4 g pro., 69 g carbo., 4 g dietary fiber, 359 mg sodium.*

APPLES 'N' CREAM PIE

Serves 8

     3 **large baking apples, peeled, cored, and sliced (5 cups)**
     1 **recipe Pastry for Double-Crust Pie**
 1½ **cups sugar**
  ¼ **cup all-purpose flour**
  ½ **teaspoon salt**
  ⅛ **teaspoon ground cinnamon**
  ½ **cup half and half *or* light cream**

Place apples in a pastry-lined 10-inch pie plate. In a medium mixing bowl stir together sugar, flour, salt, and cinnamon. Stir in cream. Pour over apples.

For top crust, roll remaining dough to about 11 inches in diameter. Cut slits or a design to allow steam to escape. Place top crust on filling. Trim top crust ½ inch beyond edge of plate. Fold top crust under bottom crust; flute edge.

Cover edge of crust with foil. Bake in a 375° oven for 25 minutes. Remove foil. Bake for 20 to 25 minutes more or till top is golden and apples are tender. Serve warm. Cover any leftover pie and store in the refrigerator.

Pastry for Double-Crust Pie: In a mixing bowl stir together 2 cups *all-purpose flour* and ½ teaspoon *salt*. Cut in ⅔ cup *shortening* till pieces are the size of small peas. Sprinkle 1 tablespoon *cold water* over part of mixture; gently toss with a fork. Push to side of bowl. Repeat with more water (5 to 6 tablespoons) till all is moistened. Divide dough in half. Form each half into a ball.

On a lightly floured surface flatten one ball of dough with hands. Roll dough from center to edges, forming a circle about 13 inches in diameter. Wrap pastry around rolling pin. Unroll onto a 10-inch pie plate. Ease pastry into pie plate, being careful not to stretch pastry. Trim pastry even with rim of pie plate. For top crust, continue as directed above.

Per serving: *484 cal., 19 g fat (5 g sat. fat), 6 mg chol., 4 g pro., 75 g carbo., 2 g dietary fiber, 275 mg sodium.*

This pie has been in our family as long as I can remember. When I was young, my mom, sister, and I would head for the apple orchard first thing on a fall morning and pick several bushels of apples. We always made this luscious pie when we got home.

—Jennifer Peterson

PEACHES AND ICE CREAM TARTS

After spotting a mouth-watering picture of peach tarts with phyllo crust in a magazine, I conjured up my own version. It's so easy, now my husband enjoys making these tasty tarts on weekends for a family treat.

—Kristi Fuller

Serves 4

> 4 **sheets frozen phyllo dough (18x12-inch rectangles), thawed**
> 2 **tablespoons margarine** *or* **butter, melted**
> 4 **peaches, baking apples,** *or* **pears, peeled and coarsely chopped**
> 6 **tablespoons amaretto**
> 2 **tablespoons margarine** *or* **butter**
> 2 **tablespoons brown sugar**
> ½ **teaspoon ground cinnamon**
> ¼ **teaspoon ground nutmeg**
> **Vanilla ice cream**
> 4 **tablespoons sliced almonds** *or* **chopped pecans (optional)**

Grease four 4¼x1-inch pie plates or four 6-ounce custard cups. Set aside. Unfold phyllo dough. Place one sheet of phyllo on a waxed-paper-lined cutting board; brush lightly with some of the 2 tablespoons melted margarine or butter (remove 1 sheet of the phyllo at a time and keep the remaining sheets of phyllo covered with a damp paper towel). Using a sharp knife, cut the sheet of phyllo into nine 6x4-inch rectangles. Gently press the 9 rectangles into the bottom of *one* pie plate or custard cup so the entire plate or cup is covered. Repeat with the remaining phyllo, melted margarine or butter, and plates or cups. Bake in a 350° oven for 10 to 15 minutes or till golden brown. Cool. Remove from pie plates or custard cups.

For sauce, in a medium saucepan combine: peaches, apples, or pears; *2 tablespoons* of the amaretto; the remaining margarine or butter; brown sugar; cinnamon; and nutmeg. Cook and stir over medium heat till margarine or butter is melted; cover. Reduce heat to low and simmer for 10 to 15 minutes or till fruit is tender. Remove from heat. Stir in remaining amaretto. To serve, place a scoop of ice cream in each phyllo cup and ladle warm fruit atop. Sprinkle each with *1 tablespoon* of the almonds or pecans, if desired.

Per serving: *455 cal., 19 g fat (6 g sat. fat), 30 mg chol., 5 g pro., 59 g carbo., 2 g dietary fiber, 287 mg sodium.*

CHOCO-CHERRY TARTS

Serves 24

> 1 **cup all-purpose flour**
> ⅓ **cup sugar**
> ¼ **cup unsweetened cocoa powder**
> ½ **cup margarine *or* butter**
> 2 **to 3 tablespoons cold water**
> 1 **21-ounce can cherry pie filling**
> **Whipped cream**
> **Sliced almonds (optional)**

For pastry, in a medium mixing bowl combine flour, sugar, and cocoa powder. With a pastry blender or two forks, cut in margarine or butter till pieces are size of small peas. Sprinkle with water, *1 tablespoon* at a time, tossing till moistened. Form into a ball.

Divide pastry into 24 small balls. Place each in an ungreased 1¾-inch muffin cup; press dough evenly against bottom and sides. Spoon a generous *tablespoon* of cherry pie filling into each muffin cup.

Bake in a 325° oven for 15 to 18 minutes or till done. Cool 30 minutes in pans. Remove from pans; cool completely on wire racks. At serving time, dollop each tart with whipped cream. If desired, top with 2 or 3 almond slices.

Per serving: *141 cal., 10 g fat (4 g sat. fat), 20 mg chol., 1 g pro., 14 g carbo., 1 g dietary fiber, 58 mg sodium.*

I never met a chocolate dessert I didn't like. If they're easy to make, like this one, all the better. These mini, cherry-filled chocolate pies were the first recipe my daughter called home for after she was married.

—Janet Figg

CUSTARD RUM TORTA

Serves 8

I first made this recipe in high school, trying to help a favored aunt impress her suitor. It worked—he proposed. (Either he liked my aunt or he liked my dessert.) I made it again to impress a college boyfriend. (He loved the cake—I don't think he liked me.) And, I made it more recently for a couple celebrating their 38th wedding anniversary. Serving this dessert doesn't always have to be inspired by love, but people seem to love it.

—Lisa Kingsley

- 4 **cups whole strawberries, washed**
- 6 **eggs, at room temperature**
- ¾ **cup sugar**
- 1 **teaspoon vanilla**
- ⅔ **cup all-purpose flour**
- ⅓ **cup cake flour**
- 2 **cups milk**
- 3 **tablespoons sugar**
- ½ **teaspoon vanilla**
- 4 **egg yolks**
- 2 **cups whipping cream**
- ¼ **cup powdered sugar**
- ½ **cup white rum**

Reserve 6 whole berries, stems intact. Thinly slice remaining berries.

Grease and flour a 9-inch springform pan; set aside. In a large mixer bowl beat the 6 eggs, the ¾ cup sugar, and the 1 teaspoon vanilla with an electric mixer on medium-high speed about 5 minutes or till thick and lemon-colored. In a medium bowl combine flours and ⅛ teaspoon *salt.* Sift flour mixture, *one-fourth* at a time, over the egg mixture, folding gently after each addition. Pour batter into prepared pan. Bake in a 325° oven 35 minutes or till top springs back when gently pressed. Loosen from pan; cool completely.

For custard, in a saucepan combine milk and the 3 tablespoons sugar. Cook and stir over low heat till sugar is dissolved. In a large bowl whisk the 4 egg yolks slightly; slowly add *⅓ cup* of warm milk mixture, whisking constantly. Stir egg mixture into remaining milk mixture. Cook and stir till custard mixture just coats back of a metal spoon. Remove from heat. Stir in the ½ teaspoon vanilla. Quickly cool custard by placing the saucepan in a bowl of ice water for 1 to 2 minutes, stirring constantly. Cover; chill for 2 to 24 hours.

In a chilled mixer bowl combine cream and powdered sugar. Beat with chilled beaters of an electric mixer till soft peaks form. Slice cake in *thirds,* horizontally. Sprinkle *one-third* of the rum over bottom layer. Spread top with *half* of the custard. Top with *half* of the sliced strawberries. Place middle cake layer on top and repeat rum, custard, and strawberries. Top with remaining cake layer; sprinkle with remaining rum. Frost cake with *two-thirds* of the whipped cream. Fill pastry bag, fitted with a large tip, with remaining whipped cream. Pipe borders around bottom and top rims of cake. Arrange berries atop cake. Chill 2 to 8 hours before serving.

Per serving: *739 cal., 52 g fat (30 g sat. fat), 435 mg chol., 12 g pro., 50 g carbo., 2 g dietary fiber, 160 mg sodium.*

One look at this three-layer, fresh strawberry cake and you'll be convinced it's incredibly luscious. One forkful will confirm it.

CANNOLI CAKE

Serves 16

   2 tablespoons untinted pistachio nuts, finely chopped
Green food coloring
   3 eggs
1½ cups sugar
1½ cups all-purpose flour
1½ teaspoons baking powder
 ¾ cup milk
  1 tablespoon margarine *or* butter
 ¾ cup sugar
  3 tablespoons cornstarch
 ¾ cup milk
  1 15-ounce carton ricotta cheese (1¾ cups)
1½ teaspoons vanilla
 ½ cup miniature semisweet chocolate pieces
 ¾ cup shortening
  1 teaspoon vanilla
  3 cups sifted powdered sugar
Milk

Tint pistachio nuts with a few drops of green food coloring; set aside. In a large mixer bowl beat eggs with an electric mixer on medium-high speed for 4 to 5 minutes or till thick and lemon-colored. Gradually beat in the 1½ cups sugar; beat 1 minute more. Combine flour and baking powder. Add to egg mixture. Stir just till combined. In a small saucepan heat the first ¾ cup milk and margarine or butter just till margarine or butter is melted. Stir into egg mixture. Pour batter into 2 foil-lined 9x1½-inch round baking pans. Bake in a 350° oven 25 to 30 minutes. Cool cake layers completely. Remove cake layers from pans. Split layers in half horizontally.

For filling, in a small saucepan combine ¾ cup sugar and cornstarch. Slowly stir in remaining ¾ cup milk. Cook and stir till thickened and bubbly. Remove from heat. Cover surface with waxed paper; cool without stirring. In a small mixer bowl beat ricotta till creamy. Stir in cooled cornstarch mixture and 1½ teaspoons vanilla. Stir in chocolate pieces. For frosting, in a small mixer bowl beat shortening and 1 teaspoon vanilla. Beat in powdered sugar just till mixed. Stir in *2 tablespoons* milk. Thin with additional milk, if necessary, to make of spreading consistency. Place 1 cake layer on a serving plate. Spread *one-third* of the ricotta filling over layer. Repeat with 2 more cake layers and the remaining filling. Top with remaining cake layer. Frost top and sides of cake with frosting. Sprinkle nuts around cake edge. Chill 2 to 24 hours.

Per serving: *426 cal., 18 g fat (7 g sat. fat), 56 mg chol., 7 g pro., 62 g carbo., 1 g dietary fiber, 85 mg sodium.*

CARROT-PINEAPPLE CAKE

Serves 9

1½ **cups all-purpose flour**
¾ **cup sugar**
 1 **teaspoon baking powder**
 1 **teaspoon ground cinnamon**
½ **teaspoon baking soda**
¼ **teaspoon salt**
 1 **8¼-ounce can crushed pineapple (juice pack)**
 1 **cup finely shredded carrot**
½ **cup cooking oil**
 1 **egg**
 2 **egg whites**
 1 **teaspoon vanilla**
 1 **recipe Cream Cheese Frosting**

Grease and lightly flour an 8x8x2-inch baking pan. In a large mixer bowl stir together flour, sugar, baking powder, cinnamon, baking soda, and salt. Add *undrained* pineapple, carrot, oil, egg, egg whites, and vanilla. Beat with an electric mixer on low speed till combined, then on medium speed for 2 minutes.

Pour batter into prepared pan. Bake in a 350° oven about 35 minutes or till a toothpick inserted near center comes out clean. Cool thoroughly on wire rack. Frost with Cream Cheese Frosting. Store cake, lightly covered, in the refrigerator. Let stand at room temperature about 30 minutes before serving.

Cream Cheese Frosting: In a mixer bowl beat together 2 ounces *cream cheese*, 3 tablespoons *butter*, and ½ teaspoon *vanilla* till light and fluffy. Gradually add about 1⅓ cups sifted *powdered sugar*, beating till smooth. Add more powdered sugar, if needed, to make frosting of spreading consistency.

Per serving: *394 cal., 19 g fat (6 g sat. fat), 41 mg chol., 4 g pro., 53 g carbo., 1 g dietary fiber, 213 mg sodium.*

Old-fashioned desserts like carrot cake are my family's weakness. But, preferring to keep after-dinner sweets on the light side, I experimented with a standard recipe, reducing the amount of sugar, eggs, and oil without sacrificing that great traditional taste. Now, my family doesn't even know this version is a little better for them!

—Joy Taylor

RHUBARB COBBLER CAKE

In spring, when the rhubarb patch is thriving, I slice the stalks in ½-inch pieces and freeze them in 3-cup portions. That way, I can make this heartwarming dessert year-round, even on a cold winter day. When using frozen rhubarb, let it thaw; then drain off any liquid before placing the rhubarb in the baking dish.

—Shelli McConnell

Serves 6 to 8

    3 cups sliced rhubarb
    2 tablespoons sugar
    1 cup all-purpose flour
    ¾ cup sugar
    1 teaspoon baking powder
    ¼ teaspoon salt
    ½ cup milk
    3 tablespoons margarine *or* butter, melted
    1 cup sugar
    1 tablespoon cornstarch
    1 cup boiling water
Half and half *or* light cream (optional)

Place rhubarb in a 9x9x2-inch baking dish. Sprinkle the 2 tablespoons sugar over the rhubarb.

In a medium mixing bowl stir together the flour, the ¾ cup sugar, the baking powder, and salt. Add the milk and melted margarine or butter. Stir till combined. Pour the batter over the rhubarb and spread evenly.

In a medium mixing bowl stir together the 1 cup sugar and the cornstarch. Add the boiling water and stir till sugar is dissolved. Slowly pour the mixture over the top of the batter. Bake in a 375° oven for 45 to 50 minutes or till top is golden brown. Let cool for 30 minutes. If desired, serve with half and half or cream.

Per serving: *395 cal., 6 g fat (1 g sat. fat), 2 mg chol., 3 g pro., 83 g carbo., 2 g dietary fiber, 219 mg sodium.*

CAPPUCCINO CHEESECAKE

Serves 12 to 16

- 1 8½-ounce package chocolate wafers, finely crushed
- ⅓ cup margarine *or* butter, melted
- 4 8-ounce packages cream cheese, cut into cubes
- ¼ cup half and half, light cream, *or* whipping cream
- 1½ teaspoons vanilla
- 1 cup sugar
- 5 slightly beaten eggs, at room temperature
- ¼ cup brewed espresso *or* double-strength coffee
- 1 ounce bittersweet *or* semisweet chocolate, chopped
- ¼ cup coffee liqueur
- ½ teaspoon lemon juice
- 2 ounces bittersweet *or* semisweet chocolate, melted

For crust, in a medium mixing bowl stir together crushed chocolate wafers and margarine or butter. Mix well. Spread mixture evenly into a 10-inch springform pan. Press onto bottom and up sides to form a firm, even crust. Chill crust about 5 minutes. Bake crust in a 350° oven for 5 minutes. Transfer to a wire rack; cool.

In a large mixer bowl beat cream cheese with an electric mixer on medium speed till smooth. Beat in half and half or cream and vanilla till smooth, scraping down sides of bowl as needed. Slowly add sugar and beat till smooth. Reduce to low speed. Slowly add eggs, beating on low speed just till combined. Set aside.

In a small saucepan combine espresso or coffee and the 1 ounce chocolate. Cook and stir over low heat till chocolate is completely melted. Stir in coffee liqueur. Cool.

Reserve *2½ cups* of cream cheese mixture; cover and chill. Stir chocolate mixture into remaining cream cheese mixture. Stir thoroughly. Pour chocolate mixture into crumb crust. Bake in a 350° oven 40 minutes or till sides are set (center will still be liquid). Remove reserved mixture from refrigerator 10 minutes before needed.

Carefully remove pan from oven onto a wire rack. Reduce oven temperature to 325°. Stir lemon juice into reserved cream cheese mixture. Slowly pour reserved mixture in a ring over the *outside* edge of the chocolate mixture (where chocolate mixture is set), allowing cream cheese mixture to slowly flow into center. Carefully return pan to oven. Bake for 30 to 35 minutes more or till center appears nearly set when gently shaken. Cool for 15 minutes on a wire rack. Loosen sides of cheesecake from pan. Cool for 30 minutes more; remove sides of pan. Cool completely. Chill at least 4 hours. To serve, drizzle top of whole cheesecake with melted chocolate. Or, cut cheesecake into pieces and transfer to dessert plates. With a spoon, drizzle melted chocolate atop cheesecake and onto plates. To store, chill, covered, up to 3 days.

Per serving: *561 cal., 40 g fat (20 g sat. fat), 175 mg chol., 10 g pro., 41 g carbo., 0 g dietary fiber, 454 mg sodium.*

For years, when I wanted to impress someone with my cooking (especially old boyfriends and now my husband), I have always turned to this showy, two-layer dessert. Of all the cheesecakes I've tasted, this one is still my favorite. You can make it one or two days ahead, cover, and chill.

—Lisa Holderness-Brown

DOUBLE-CHOCOLATE CHEESECAKE

Serves 12

1½ **cups finely crushed chocolate wafers**
 ⅓ **cup butter *or* margarine, melted**
 3 **8-ounce packages cream cheese, softened**
1½ **cups sugar**
 4 **squares (4 ounces) semisweet chocolate, melted and cooled**
 2 **tablespoons all-purpose flour**
 1 **teaspoon vanilla**
 4 **eggs**
 ¼ **cup milk**
 ¼ **cup vanilla-flavored pieces, melted (optional)**
 1 **square (1 ounce) semisweet chocolate**
 2 **teaspoons shortening**

For the crust, in a mixing bowl stir together crushed wafers and butter or margarine. Press mixture evenly over the bottom and 1¾ inches up sides of a 9-inch springform pan. Place the pan in a shallow baking pan.

For filling, in a large mixer bowl beat cream cheese, sugar, the 4 squares melted chocolate, flour, and vanilla till well mixed. Add eggs all at once, then beat with an electric mixer on low speed just till mixed. *Do not overbeat.* Stir in milk. Pour filling into the crust.

Bake in a 350° oven about 45 minutes or till center appears nearly set when gently shaken. Cool on a wire rack for 5 to 10 minutes. Loosen sides of cheesecake from pan. Cool about 30 minutes. Remove sides of pan. Cover and chill 4 to 24 hours.

For star design, if desired, place melted vanilla-flavored pieces in a pastry bag fitted with a small round tip or in a small plastic bag with a corner snipped. Pipe melted vanilla-flavored pieces into stars atop cheesecake. In a small saucepan melt the 1 square chocolate and shortening over low heat. Pipe into stars as directed above or drizzle over top of cheesecake. Chill till chocolate is set.

Per serving: *524 cal., 34 g fat (19 g sat. fat), 147 mg chol., 8 g pro., 49 g carbo., 0 g dietary fiber, 369 mg sodium.*

This special-occasion dessert appears at many of my dinner gatherings. Once I even dropped it as I pulled it out of the oven. When I apologetically described the would-have-been dessert to my guests, they insisted on eating it anyway. It still tasted great, even though it didn't look so good!

—Diana McMillen

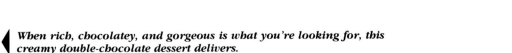

When rich, chocolatey, and gorgeous is what you're looking for, this creamy double-chocolate dessert delivers.

COCONUT CHEESECAKE

A friend of mine is just crazy about coconut. Every year for her birthday, I make her this dreamy, double-coconut cheesecake.

—Diane Yanney

Serves 12 to 16

1¾ cups flaked coconut
1 tablespoon margarine *or* butter, softened
3 8-ounce packages cream cheese, softened
1 cup sugar
2 tablespoons all-purpose flour
¼ teaspoon coconut extract *or* vanilla
⅛ teaspoon salt
3 eggs
¼ cup milk
1 8-ounce carton dairy sour cream
1 tablespoon sugar

Toast *1 cup* of the coconut in a 350° oven for 10 to 12 minutes; stir occasionally. Reserve *¼ cup* of the toasted coconut for the topping.

Grease the bottom and sides of an 8- or 9-inch springform pan with the softened margarine or butter. Press the remaining toasted coconut on the bottom of the pan. Press the untoasted coconut *1¾ inches* up sides of the pan.

For filling, in a large mixer bowl combine cream cheese, the 1 cup sugar, flour, coconut extract or vanilla, and salt. Beat with an electric mixer on medium-high speed till fluffy. Add the eggs, all at once, beating at low speed just till blended. *Do not overbeat.* Stir in the milk. Pour into coconut-lined pan. Bake in a 375° oven about 45 minutes or till center appears nearly set when gently shaken.

Meanwhile, for topping, combine the sour cream and 1 tablespoon sugar. Spread atop baked cheesecake. Cool on wire rack. Chill. To serve, sprinkle with reserved toasted coconut.

Per serving: *391 cal., 30 g fat (19 g sat. fat), 124 mg chol., 7 g pro., 26 g carbo., 1 g dietary fiber, 232 mg sodium.*

PEANUT BUTTER ICE CREAM TORTE

Serves 20

- 1¾ **cups finely crushed graham crackers**
- ½ **cup finely chopped pecans**
- ½ **cup margarine *or* butter, melted**
- ¼ **cup sugar**
- ½ **gallon vanilla *or* butter pecan ice cream**
- 1 **8-ounce carton frozen whipped dessert topping, thawed**
- 1 **cup creamy peanut butter**
- 1 **5½-ounce can chocolate syrup**

For crust, in a medium mixing bowl combine finely crushed graham crackers, pecans, melted margarine or butter, and sugar. Reserve *½ cup* of the mixture. Press remaining crumb mixture into a 13x9x2-inch pan.

In an large bowl stir ice cream to soften. Stir in thawed topping and peanut butter. Mix well. Spread evenly over crumb crust. Drizzle with chocolate syrup and sprinkle with reserved crumbs. Freeze several hours or overnight. To serve, let stand for 10 minutes before cutting into squares.

Per serving: *385 cal., 23 g fat (8 g sat. fat), 24 mg chol., 7 g pro., 42 g carbo., 2 g dietary fiber, 247 mg sodium.*

In search of a novel recipe my kids would like, I created this layered frozen torte. To my surprise, my husband, who usually doesn't like dessert, finished every bite, too.

—Maryellyn Krantz

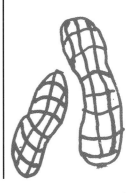

SWEDISH CURRANT MERINGUE SOUFFLÉ

Serves 12

Fresh red and black currants are as easy to find in Europe as strawberries are in the U.S. The limited supply of fresh currants in this country shows up at local farmers' markets and some upscale supermarkets during the summer months. This is the ultimate after-dinner dessert—tart bursts of fresh currants contrasted with sweet, pillow-soft meringue and cream. Believe me, it's worth your market search!

—Nancy Byal

4 egg whites, at room temperature
1½ teaspoons lemon juice
1 teaspoon vanilla
1 cup sugar
3 cups fresh red currants *or* red raspberries
3 cups whipping cream
3 tablespoons sugar
1 teaspoon vanilla
Powdered sugar

Preheat oven to 450°. Grease the bottom of a 2-quart soufflé dish. Set aside. In a large mixer bowl beat egg whites, lemon juice, and the first teaspoon vanilla with an electric mixer on medium speed for 3 to 4 minutes or till soft peaks form (tips curl).

Gradually beat in the 1 cup sugar, 1 tablespoon at a time, beating on high speed till stiff peaks form (tips stand straight) and sugar is almost dissolved (about 10 minutes). Turn meringue mixture into prepared dish; spread evenly on bottom and up sides to within one inch of top edge of dish. Place in preheated oven. Turn oven off. Let meringue dry in oven with door closed for at least 8 hours or overnight.

Eight to 24 hours ahead of serving time, rinse currants or berries and drain thoroughly on paper towels. In a chilled large mixer bowl beat whipping cream on low speed till soft peaks form (tips curl). Add the 3 tablespoons sugar and the remaining vanilla; beat till stiff peaks form (tips stand straight). Fold in *2 cups* currants or berries. Chill remaining fruit. Spoon whipped cream mixture atop meringue, covering entire meringue. Cover and chill 8 to 24 hours.

To serve, garnish top of dessert with remaining fruit. Sift a little powdered sugar lightly over fruit. Spoon the soufflé into dishes, being sure to spoon into softened meringue.

Per serving: *305 cal., 22 g fat (14 g sat. fat), 82 mg chol., 3 g pro., 26 g carbo., 1 g dietary fiber, 42 mg sodium.*

TOASTED BREAD PUDDING

Serves 4

    4 ¾-inch-thick slices French bread
Margarine *or* **butter**
    2 teaspoons sugar
    ¼ teaspoon ground cinnamon
    4 beaten eggs
    2 cups milk
    ⅓ cup sugar
    ½ teaspoon vanilla

Lightly spread both sides of bread slices with margarine or butter. Place bread slices on the unheated rack of a broiler pan; broil 4 inches from the heat till golden brown, turning once. Place *one* slice of toasted bread in *each* of four 10-ounce individual casseroles or 10-ounce custard cups.

Combine the 2 teaspoons sugar and cinnamon; set aside. In a medium mixing bowl beat together eggs, milk, the ⅓ cup sugar, and the vanilla with a rotary beater. Pour egg mixture evenly over bread slices in individual casseroles or custard cups. Sprinkle sugar-cinnamon mixture evenly over bread slices. Bake in a 325° oven for 30 to 35 minutes or till a knife inserted near the center comes out clean. Cool slightly before serving.

Per serving: *358 cal., 15 g fat (4 g sat. fat), 224 mg chol., 14 g pro., 43 g carbo., 1 g dietary fiber, 392 mg sodium.*

After enjoying a heavenly bread pudding in a French restaurant, I modified a basic recipe to make this more elegant version. It's even better than the pricey restaurant recipe!

—Sharyl Heiken

FRUIT PIZZA

This dessert pizza is super for brunches or dessert buffets. The fresh fruit looks so gorgeous it can serve as the centerpiece. Plus, to save time, you can bake the cookie dough crust the day before.

—Lois White

Serves 16

  1 **roll (20 ounces) refrigerated sugar cookie dough**
  1 **8-ounce container soft-style cream cheese**
  ¼ **cup sugar**
  ½ **teaspoon vanilla**
  1 **banana, peeled and sliced**
Lemon juice
  2 **kiwi fruit, peeled and sliced**
  1 **cup fresh strawberries, halved**
  ½ **cup fresh blueberries**
  ½ **cup orange marmalade *or* peach preserves**
  2 **tablespoons water**

For cookie crust, press cookie dough evenly onto a lightly greased 12-inch pizza pan. Prick with the tines of a fork. Bake in a 375° oven for 10 to 12 minutes or till golden. Cool.

In a small bowl stir together cream cheese, sugar, and vanilla till smooth. Spread mixture evenly over cooled crust. Toss banana slices with lemon juice to prevent browning. Arrange banana slices, kiwi fruit slices, halved strawberries, and blueberries atop cream cheese mixture. In a small bowl stir together marmalade and water. Spoon over fruit. Chill for 1 hour or till serving time.

Per serving: *280 cal., 14 g fat (4 g sat. fat), 36 mg chol., 3 g pro., 38 g carbo., 1 g dietary fiber, 244 mg sodium.*

FRESH-FRUIT DIP

Serves 8

> 2 tablespoons sugar
> ⅛ teaspoon ground cinnamon
> ⅛ teaspoon ground nutmeg
> Dash ground allspice
> Dash salt
> 1 cup dairy sour cream
> ½ teaspoon vanilla
> ⅛ teaspoon rum extract
> Sliced bananas, strawberries, grapes, pineapple,
>   pears, *and/or* apples

Combine sugar, cinnamon, nutmeg, allspice, and salt. Stir in sour cream, vanilla, and rum extract. Mix well. Cover and chill for 2 to 4 hours. Serve with fresh fruit.

Per serving of dip: *74 cal., 6 g fat (4 g sat. fat), 13 mg chol., 1 g pro., 4 g carbo., 0 g dietary fiber, 32 mg sodium.*

ROCKY ROAD BARK

Makes 36 pieces

> 16 ounces chocolate-flavored candy coating
> ½ cup peanut butter
> 2 cups crisp rice cereal
> 1 cup peanuts
> 1 cup tiny marshmallows

In a 3-quart saucepan combine candy coating and peanut butter. Cook and stir over low heat till coating is melted. Remove from heat; stir in cereal, peanuts, and marshmallows till coated. Drop by spoonfuls onto a foil-lined baking sheet. (Or, spread in a foil-lined 8x8x2-inch pan.) Chill for a few minutes till set. Cut into squares (if in pan).

Per serving: *121 cal., 7 g fat (4 g sat. fat), 0 mg chol., 2 g pro., 13 g carbo., 1 g dietary fiber, 55 mg sodium.*

A cookie baker's choice selection:
Rolled Sugar Cookies (page 130),
Chocolate Turtle Cookies (page 129),
Kringla (page 128), and Ginger
Cookies (page 131).

COOKIES BY THE DOZEN

Baking cookies after work hours is an activity that thrives in our home kitchens. We love the mouth-watering aroma that wafts from the kitchen as the cookies bake. Biting into a still-warm crisp round or chewy bar adds another touch of heaven. Enjoy the cream of our cookie crop in this chapter, from homey gingersnaps to festive Norwegian *kringla*.

KRINGLA

These Scandinavian figure-8 cookies taste like soft animal crackers. Store them overnight for a soft, more even texture. They're pictured on page 126.

—Jennifer Peterson

Makes 48

4½ **cups all-purpose flour**
1 **teaspoon baking soda**
1 **egg**
1¾ **cups sugar**
1 **8-ounce carton dairy sour cream**
½ **cup milk**
2 **tablespoons butter** *or* **margarine, melted**
2 **teaspoons aniseed, crushed,** *or* ¼ **teaspoon oil of anise**
Unsweetened cocoa powder (optional)

In medium mixing bowl stir together flour and baking soda; set aside. In a large mixing bowl combine egg, sugar, sour cream, milk, butter or margarine, and aniseed or oil of anise; beat with an electric mixer on medium to high speed about 30 seconds or till combined. Add flour mixture to egg mixture; beat on medium speed just till combined, scraping the sides of the bowl occasionally. Cover and chill dough overnight or till easy to handle.

On a lightly floured surface roll 1 rounded tablespoon of chilled dough into a 9-inch-long rope; shape the rope into a figure 8. Repeat with remaining dough.

Arrange pieces of shaped dough about 2 inches apart on a greased baking sheet. Position one oven rack about 5 inches from the broiler. (The second rack should be in the center of the oven.) Place one cookie sheet on the lower rack. Bake in a 400° oven for 4 minutes. Move the cookie sheet to the upper rack. Broil cookies about 5 inches from the heat about 1 minute or till light brown. (Return oven to "bake" and allow oven to cool to 400° before baking the next batch.)

Remove cookies from cookie sheet; cool completely on a wire rack. If desired, sprinkle cooled cookies with unsweetened cocoa powder.

Per serving: *88 cal., 2 g fat (1 g sat. fat), 8 mg chol., 2 g pro., 17 g carbo., 0 g dietary fiber, 27 mg sodium.*

CHOCOLATE TURTLE COOKIES

Makes 40

⅓ cup margarine *or* butter
2 squares (2 ounces) unsweetened chocolate
1 cup all-purpose flour
½ teaspoon baking powder
2 eggs
¾ cup sugar
1 teaspoon vanilla
1 recipe Chocolate Glaze
Chopped pecans *or* walnuts

In a small, heavy saucepan combine margarine or butter and chocolate; melt over medium heat, stirring occasionally. Cool to room temperature.

Meanwhile, in a small mixing bowl stir together flour and baking powder; set aside. In a medium mixing bowl combine eggs, sugar, and vanilla; beat with an electric mixer on medium to high speed about 30 seconds or till combined. Add flour mixture to egg mixture; beat on medium speed just till combined, scraping the sides of the bowl occasionally. Stir in the cooled chocolate mixture.

Heat a standard-size waffle iron to medium heat. Drop batter from a rounded teaspoon onto the middle of each section of the waffle iron. Close the lid and bake for 1 minute. Using a fork, loosen and remove the cookies. Cool cookies completely on a wire rack. Frost with Chocolate Glaze. Sprinkle with chopped nuts.

Chocolate Glaze: In a medium mixing bowl stir together 2 cups *sifted powdered sugar* and ½ cup *unsweetened cocoa powder*. Stir in enough *milk* (4 to 6 tablespoons) to make a glaze of spreading consistency.

Per serving: *81 cal., 4 g fat (1 g sat. fat), 11 mg chol., 1 g pro., 12 g carbo., 1 g dietary fiber, 26 mg sodium.*

A great kid's cookie! Crisp waffle ends poke from under the shiny chocolate glaze, making these bite-size sweets look a little like turtles. Pictured on page 126.

—Lois White

ROLLED SUGAR COOKIES

My mother's cutout cookies have always been a favorite. They're not as sweet as some, and boy, are they nice and chewy. They taste delicious plain, but you can dress them up for special occasions with colored frostings and painted designs. Pictured on page 126.

—Colleen Weeden

Makes 48

2½ **cups all-purpose flour**
1 **teaspoon baking soda**
1 **teaspoon cream of tartar**
1 **cup butter** *or* **margarine, softened**
½ **cup sifted powdered sugar**
1 **egg**
½ **teaspoon vanilla**
½ **teaspoon almond extract**
1 **recipe Vanilla Glaze (optional)**
Food coloring (optional)

In a medium mixing bowl stir together flour, baking soda, and cream of tartar; set aside. In a medium mixing bowl combine butter or margarine and powdered sugar; beat with an electric mixer on medium to high speed till fluffy. Add egg, vanilla, and almond extract; beat on medium speed till combined. Add flour mixture to egg mixture; beat on medium speed just till combined, scraping the sides of the bowl occasionally. Divide the dough in half. Cover and chill about 2 hours or till easy to handle.

On a lightly floured surface roll each portion of chilled dough to ¼-inch thickness. Using cookie cutters, cut dough into desired shapes. Arrange cutouts about 1 inch apart on greased cookie sheets.

Bake in a 375° oven for 7 to 8 minutes or till golden. Remove cookies from cookie sheet; cool completely on a wire rack. If desired, decorate cooled cookies with plain or colored Vanilla Glaze and paint with food coloring.

Vanilla Glaze: In a medium mixing bowl stir together 2 cups *sifted powdered sugar* and ½ teaspoon *vanilla*. Stir in enough *milk* (2 to 4 tablespoons) to make a glaze of spreading consistency. If desired, stir in a few drops food coloring.

Per serving: *63 cal., 4 g fat (2 g sat. fat), 15 mg chol., 1 g pro., 6 g carbo., 0 g dietary fiber, 55 mg sodium.*

Editor's note: *To paint flowers or designs on the glaze, use a small, clean paint brush dipped in food coloring.*

GINGER COOKIES

Makes 48

2¾ cups all-purpose flour
2 teaspoons cream of tartar
1 teaspoon baking soda
1 teaspoon ground ginger
½ teaspoon salt
1 cup unsalted butter
¾ cup packed brown sugar
¾ cup sugar
2 eggs
1 teaspoon vanilla
½ cup finely chopped stem (crystallized) ginger

In a medium mixing bowl stir together flour, cream of tartar, baking soda, ground ginger, and salt; set aside. In a large mixing bowl combine butter and sugars; beat with an electric mixer on medium to high speed till fluffy. Add eggs and vanilla; beat on medium speed till combined. Add flour mixture to egg mixture; beat on medium speed till combined, scraping the sides of the bowl occasionally. Stir in the stem ginger. Cover and chill the dough about 1 hour or till easy to handle.

On a lightly floured surface shape the chilled dough into 1-inch balls. Arrange balls at least 3 inches apart on an ungreased cookie sheet. (The cookies will spread during baking.) Bake in a 375° oven for 8 to 10 minutes or till cookies are pale gold. Remove cookies from cookie sheet; cool completely on a wire rack.

Per serving: *94 cal., 4 g fat (2 g sat. fat), 19 mg chol., 1 g pro., 13 g carbo., 0 g dietary fiber, 53 mg sodium.*

Editor's note: *You can find crystallized ginger in the spice section of the supermarket.*

Ginger is a favorite spice in our office, so there was much ado when the mailman brought us a box of stem ginger biscuits. When the yummy, buttery cookies were gone, I developed my own version. These cookies are especially good with a cup of tea, fruit sorbet, or ice cream. Pictured on page 126.

—Susan Sarao-Westmoreland

COCONUT-WHEAT COOKIES

My mother-in-law gave me this cookie recipe, my husband's favorite, as a wedding present. Use the shorter baking time if you like your cookies chewy, the longer baking time if you like them crisp.

—Nancy Byal

Makes 60

 2¼ **cups all-purpose flour**
   1 **teaspoon baking powder**
  ½ **teaspoon baking soda**
  ½ **teaspoon salt**
   1 **cup shortening**
   1 **cup sugar**
   1 **cup packed brown sugar**
   2 **eggs**
   1 **teaspoon vanilla**
   2 **cups wheat flake cereal**
   1 **cup coconut**

In a small mixing bowl stir together flour, baking powder, baking soda, and salt; set aside. In a large mixing bowl beat shortening and sugars with an electric mixer on medium to high speed till fluffy. Add eggs and vanilla; beat on medium speed till combined. Add flour mixture to egg mixture; beat on low speed just till combined, scraping the sides of the bowl occasionally. Stir in cereal and coconut.

Drop dough from a rounded tablespoon about 2 inches apart onto a greased cookie sheet. Bake in 375° oven for 8 to 10 minutes or till golden. Cool on the cookie sheet for 1 minute. Remove cookies from cookie sheet and cool completely on a wire rack.

Per serving: *86 cal., 4 g fat (1 g sat. fat), 7 mg chol., 1 g pro., 12 g carbo., 0 g dietary fiber, 43 mg sodium.*

GINGERSNAPS

Makes 60

2 cups all-purpose flour
2 teaspoons baking soda
1 teaspoon ground cinnamon
1 teaspoon ground cloves
1 teaspoon ground ginger
¼ teaspoon salt
¾ cup margarine *or* butter
1 cup sugar
1 egg
¼ cup molasses
1 teaspoon vanilla
Sugar

In a small mixing bowl stir together flour, baking soda, cinnamon, cloves, ginger, and salt; set aside. In a medium mixing bowl beat margarine or butter and sugar with an electric mixer on medium to high speed till fluffy. Add egg, molasses, and vanilla; beat till combined. Add flour mixture to egg mixture; beat on medium speed till combined. Cover and chill the dough at least 1 hour.

Shape the chilled dough into balls, about 1 inch in diameter. Roll in sugar; arrange balls about 2 inches apart on an ungreased cookie sheet. Using the bottom of a glass, flatten balls to about ¼-inch thickness, dipping the glass in sugar for each cookie. Bake in a 375° oven for 8 to 10 minutes or till done. Remove cookies from cookie sheet and cool completely on a wire rack.

Per serving: *53 cal., 2 g fat (0 g sat. fat), 4 mg chol., 1 g pro., 7 g carbo., 0 g dietary fiber, 65 mg sodium.*

Use a glass with a flat bottom to press the balls of cookie dough before baking. Keep dipping the glass bottom in sugar, or the dough may stick to the glass.

—Joyce Trollope

THE GREATEST PEANUT BUTTER COOKIES

*Here's a cookie recipe
that's worthy of its
name. Each cookie
shouts PEANUT BUTTER
when you bite into it!*

—Diana McMillen

Makes 50

2½ **cups all-purpose flour**
  1 **teaspoon baking soda**
  1 **cup shortening**
  1 **cup peanut butter**
  1 **cup sugar**
  1 **cup packed brown sugar**
  2 **eggs**
  1 **teaspoon vanilla**
Sugar

    In a medium mixing bowl stir together flour and baking soda; set aside. In a medium mixing bowl beat the shortening and peanut butter with an electric mixer on medium to high speed for 30 seconds or till combined. Add the sugars; beat till fluffy. Add eggs and vanilla; beat on medium speed till combined. Add the flour mixture to the egg mixture; beat on medium speed till combined, scraping the sides of the bowl occasionally.

    On a lightly floured surface shape the dough into 1- to 1½-inch balls. Arrange balls 2 inches apart on an ungreased cookie sheet. Using the tines of a fork dipped in additional sugar, flatten balls to about ½-inch thickness by pressing the fork in 2 directions to form crisscross marks. *(Or,* use a small meat mallet for a different pattern.) Bake in a 375° oven for 10 to 12 minutes or till done. Cool on the cookie sheet for 1 minute. Then remove cookies from cookie sheet and cool completely on a wire rack.

Per serving: *124 cal., 7 g fat (2 sat. fat), 9 mg chol., 2 g pro., 14 g carbo., 0 g dietary fiber, 46 mg sodium.*

Editor's note: *I use a small restaurant-style ice cream scoop (it holds about 2 tablespoons) to drop the dough onto the baking sheets.*

EGGNOG COOKIES

Makes 60

2 cups all-purpose flour
1 cup sugar
¾ teaspoon baking powder
¼ teaspoon salt
¼ teaspoon ground nutmeg *or* cardamom
⅔ cup margarine *or* butter
1 egg
¼ cup eggnog *or* light cream
½ cup finely crushed rum- *or* butterscotch-flavored hard candies
1 recipe Eggnog Glaze
Yellow colored sugar

In a medium mixing bowl stir together flour, sugar, baking powder, salt, and nutmeg or cardamom. Cut in margarine or butter till mixture resembles coarse crumbs. Make a well in the center. In a small mixing bowl beat egg slightly with a fork. Stir in ¼ cup eggnog. Add eggnog mixture all at once to flour mixture. Using a fork, stir gently just till moistened. Cover and chill dough about 2 hours or till easy to handle.

On a well-floured surface roll dough to ¼-inch thickness. Using large cookie cutters, cut dough into desired shapes. Using smaller cutters, cut smaller shapes from the inside of the larger shapes, rerolling trimmings. Arrange cutouts about 1 inch apart on a foil-lined cookie sheet. Sprinkle crushed candies into holes of cutouts. Bake cookies in a 375° oven for 8 to 12 minutes or till golden. Cool on the cookie sheet for 5 minutes. Then, remove cookies and foil and cool completely on a wire rack. When cool, carefully remove foil. Spread the top of each cookie with some of the glaze. Sprinkle with colored sugar.

Eggnog Glaze: In a small mixing bowl stir together 1 cup sifted *powdered sugar,* 10 drops *rum extract,* and enough *eggnog* (1 to 2 tablespoons) to make a glaze of spreading consistency.

Per serving: *61 cal., 2 g fat (0 g sat. fat), 4 mg chol., 1 g pro., 10 g carbo., 0 g dietary fiber, 39 mg sodium.*

What could be better than a favorite holiday drink made into a cookie? Splash some eggnog and nutmeg into the dough and sprinkle the cutouts with crushed rum candies. The candies melt during baking to create a colorful and pretty stained-glass effect.

—Julia Malloy

ITALIAN FIG COOKIES

Makes 24

2½ cups all-purpose flour
⅓ cup sugar
¼ teaspoon baking powder
½ cup shortening
2 tablespoons margarine *or* butter
1 beaten egg
½ cup milk
1 8-ounce package dried figs (1½ cups)
¾ cup light raisins
¼ cup slivered almonds
¼ cup sugar
¼ cup hot water
¼ teaspoon ground cinnamon
Dash pepper
1 recipe Confectioners' Icing
Small multicolored decorative candies

In a large mixing bowl combine flour, the ⅓ cup sugar, and baking powder. Cut in shortening and margarine or butter till pieces resemble coarse crumbs. Make a well in the center. In a small mixing bowl stir together egg and milk. Add egg mixture all at once to flour mixture. Using a fork, stir just till moistened. Divide dough in half. Cover and chill 2 hours or till easy to handle.

For filling, in a food processor bowl or with the coarse blade of a food grinder, process or grind figs, raisins, and almonds till coarsely chopped. In a medium mixing bowl combine the ¼ cup sugar, hot water, cinnamon, and pepper. Stir in the fruit mixture. Let the filling stand till the dough is thoroughly chilled.

On a lightly floured surface roll *each* portion of dough into a 12-inch square. Cut *each* square into *twelve* 4x3-inch rectangles. Place a heaping tablespoon of filling along the short side of *each* rectangle. Roll up from the short side. Place rolls, seam side down, on an ungreased cookie sheet. Curve each roll slightly into a crescent shape. Snip or cut the outer edge of the curve 3 times. Bake in a 350° oven for 20 to 25 minutes or till cookies are golden. Remove cookies from cookie sheet; cool on a wire rack. Drizzle with Confectioners' Icing. Sprinkle with decorative candies.

Confectioners' Icing: In a small mixing bowl combine 1 cup sifted *powdered sugar* and ¼ teaspoon *vanilla*. Add enough *milk* (about 1 teaspoon) to make a glaze of drizzling consistency.

Per serving: *182 cal., 7 g fat (2 g sat. fat), 9 mg chol., 3 g pro., 30 g carbo., 2 g dietary fiber, 22 mg sodium.*

CHOCOLATE-BANANA BAR COOKIES

Makes 32

- 1½ **cups all-purpose flour**
- ½ **cup granulated sugar**
- ½ **cup packed brown sugar**
- ½ **teaspoon baking soda**
- ½ **teaspoon salt**
- ¼ **teaspoon baking powder**
- 2 **very ripe medium bananas, sliced (about 1½ cups)**
- ½ **cup shortening**
- 2 **eggs**
- ⅓ **cup buttermilk**
- 1 **teaspoon vanilla**
- ⅓ **cup miniature semisweet chocolate pieces**
- 1 **recipe Vanilla Icing**

In a small mixing bowl stir together flour, sugar, brown sugar, baking soda, salt, and baking powder. Add sliced bananas, shortening, eggs, buttermilk, and vanilla. Beat with an electric mixer on medium speed about 2 minutes or till smooth. Stir in the chocolate pieces.

Spread batter in a greased 13x9x2-inch baking pan. Bake in a 350° oven about 25 minutes or till a wooden toothpick comes out clean. Cool completely on a wire rack. Drizzle with Vanilla Icing. Let stand a few hours before cutting into bars or squares.

Vanilla Icing: In a small mixing bowl combine 1 cup sifted *powdered sugar,* 1 teaspoon *light corn syrup,* ½ teaspoon *vanilla,* and enough *milk* (about 4 teaspoons) to make an icing of drizzling consistency.

Per serving: *109 cal., 4 g fat (1 g sat. fat), 14 mg chol., 1 g pro., 17 g carbo., 0 g dietary fiber, 57 mg sodium.*

Remember this cakelike cookie next time your bananas get very ripe. You can cut the cookies into rectangles for bar cookies or into larger pieces for cake.

—Joyce Trollope

ORANGE-ALMOND BARS

At Christmastime, every gallon-size, shiny gold tin in Grandma's pantry concealed a different kind of buttery cookie. The tin with these bars was the one I always reached for.

—Julia Malloy

Makes 48

  ½ **cup butter** *or* **margarine**
1¾ **cups all-purpose flour**
  1 **cup sugar**
  1 **egg**
  2 **teaspoons baking powder**
  ½ **teaspoon finely shredded orange peel**
  ½ **teaspoon almond extract**
Milk
  ½ **cup sliced almonds, coarsely chopped**
  1 **recipe Orange Icing**

In a medium mixing bowl beat butter or margarine with an electric mixer on medium to high speed for 30 seconds. Add about *half* of the flour, the sugar, egg, baking powder, orange peel, and almond extract. Beat mixture till combined. Beat in the remaining flour.

Divide dough into fourths. On a lightly floured surface form each portion into a 12-inch-long roll. Place 2 rolls 4 to 5 inches apart on an ungreased cookie sheet. Flatten with hands till rolls are 3 inches wide.

Brush flattened rolls with milk; sprinkle with almonds. Bake in a 325° oven for 12 to 14 minutes or till edges are light brown. While cookies are warm, cut crosswise at a diagonal into 1-inch-wide strips. Cool cookies on a wire rack. Drizzle icing over cooled cookies.

Orange Icing: In a small mixing bowl stir together 1 cup sifted *powdered sugar* and ¼ teaspoon *almond extract.* Stir in enough orange juice (1 to 2 tablespoons) to make an icing of drizzling consistency.

Per serving: *68 cal., 3 g fat (1 g sat. fat), 10 mg chol., 1 g pro., 10 g carbo., 0 g dietary fiber, 30 mg sodium.*

OATMEAL CHOCOLATE CHIP COOKIES

Makes 60

- 1½ **cups all-purpose flour**
- 1 **teaspoon baking soda**
- 1 **cup butter** *or* **margarine**
- ¾ **cup sugar**
- ¾ **cup packed brown sugar**
- 2 **eggs**
- 1 **teaspoon vanilla**
- 3 **cups quick-cooking rolled oats**
- 1 **12-ounce package semisweet chocolate pieces**

In a small mixing bowl stir together flour and baking soda; set aside. In a large mixing bowl combine butter or margarine and sugars; beat with an electric mixer on medium to high speed about 30 seconds or till fluffy. Add eggs and vanilla; beat on medium speed till combined. Add flour mixture to egg mixture; beat on medium speed just till combined, scraping the sides of the bowl occasionally. Stir in the oats and chocolate pieces.

Drop dough from a rounded teaspoon about 2 inches apart onto an ungreased cookie sheet. Bake in a 375° oven for 10 to 12 minutes or till done. Remove cookies from the cookie sheet; cool completely on a wire rack.

Per serving: *105 cal., 6 g fat (3 g sat. fat), 15 mg chol., 1 g pro., 14 g carbo., 1 g dietary fiber, 44 mg sodium.*

My brother always pestered me to make these cookies. The problem wasn't just keeping enough on hand, but getting them baked before he'd eaten half of the dough.

—Marilyn Cornelius

SECRETS TO HAPPY BAKING

Few of us have the time to bake like we used to, let alone experiment when we bake. So we pooled together some tips to ensure that your baking experiences (no matter how frequent) are always happy times, and your baked goods, always delicious successes.

Cookie-Making Matters

Beyond a doubt, homemade cookies are America's No. 1 treat, and cookie baking, one of our all-time-favorite pastimes.

1. *Don't use soft margarine, a spread, or diet margarine.* Products other than stick butter, stick margarine, and solid shortening have a high percent of air whipped into them and may have added water, too. Unless your recipe was specially developed to use one of these lower-fat products, your cookies won't turn out right.
2. *Doughs made with 100 percent corn oil margarine require special handling.* For cutout or slice-and-bake cookies, this margarine produces a softer dough that requires special chilling. For cutout cookies, chill the dough at least five hours before you roll it out. (For slice-and-bake cookies, chill the rolls of dough in the freezer rather than in the refrigerator.)
3. *Choose cookie sheets that are shiny, heavy-gauge aluminum or nonstick.* Dark cookie sheets absorb heat faster, making it harder to avoid overbrowning the cookie bottoms.
4. *Always place your cookie dough on cool cookie sheets* so the cookies won't overspread as they bake.
5. *To mix now, bake later,* store the cookie dough (thin batters and meringue doughs excepted) in a tightly covered container in the refrigerator for up to one week or in the freezer for up to six months. Thaw frozen dough before using.

Dessert-Baking Pointers

Some baking tips are so universal they apply whether you're making homey bread pudding or pull-out-all-the-stops cheesecake.

1. *Use the right utensil.* There are measurable differences between liquid measuring cups and dry measuring cups. To avoid a failure, don't measure dry ingredients in liquid measures or liquid ingredients in dry measures.
2. *Use large eggs* for dessert recipes unless otherwise specified.
3. *Sift cake flour,* since its fine texture causes cake flour to pack down in shipping. You needn't sift all-purpose flour; simply stir it before measuring.
4. *Check your oven temperature.* It's common for oven temperatures to vary 25° up or down. Your best bet is to use an oven thermometer and adjust the setting as needed. Always preheat your oven 10 to 15 minutes before baking.

SUBSTITUTIONS FOR EMERGENCIES

INGREDIENT	SUBSTITUTION
1 tablespoon cornstarch	2 tablespoons all-purpose flour (for thickening)
1 teaspoon baking powder	½ teaspoon cream of tartar *plus* ¼ teaspoon baking soda
1 cup granulated sugar	1 cup packed brown sugar *or* 2 cups sifted powdered sugar
1 cup cake flour	1 cup *minus* 2 tablespoons all-purpose flour
1 cup light cream	1 tablespoon melted butter *plus* enough milk to make 1 cup
1 cup dairy sour cream	1 cup plain yogurt
1 cup buttermilk or sour milk	1 tablespoon lemon juice *or* vinegar *plus* enough whole milk to make 1 cup (let stand for 5 minutes before using), *or* 1 cup whole milk *plus* 1¾ teaspoons cream of tartar, *or* 1 cup plain yogurt.
1 cup honey	1¼ cups sugar *plus* ¼ cup liquid
1 cup corn syrup	1 cup sugar *plus* ¼ cup liquid
1 cup dark corn syrup	¾ cup light corn syrup *plus* ¼ cup molasses, *or* 1 cup light corn syrup
1 cup molasses	1 cup honey
1 square (1 ounce) unsweetened chocolate	3 tablespoons unsweetened cocoa powder *plus* 1 tablespoon shortening *or* cooking oil, *or* one 1-ounce envelope premelted unsweetened chocolate product
6 squares (6 ounces) semisweet chocolate	6 ounces semisweet chocolate pieces, *or* 6 tablespoons unsweetened cocoa powder *plus* ¼ cup sugar and ¼ cup shortening.
2 cups tomato sauce	¾ cup tomato paste *plus* 1 cup water
¼ cup fine dry bread crumbs	¾ cup soft bread crumbs, *or* ¼ cup cracker crumbs, *or* ¼ cup cornflake crumbs, *or* ⅔ cup rolled oats
1 clove garlic	½ teaspoon bottled minced garlic *or* ⅛ teaspoon garlic powder
1 tablespoon prepared mustard	½ teaspoon dry mustard *plus* 2 teaspoons vinegar
1 teaspoon apple pie spice	½ teaspoon ground cinnamon *plus* ¼ teaspoon ground nutmeg, ⅛ teaspoon ground allspice, and dash ground ginger
1 teaspoon pumpkin pie spice	½ teaspoon ground cinnamon *plus* ¼ teaspoon ground ginger, ¼ teaspoon ground allspice, and ⅛ teaspoon ground nutmeg

WEIGHTS AND MEASURES

3 teaspoons	1 tablespoon	1 tablespoon	½ fluid ounce
4 tablespoons	¼ cup	1 cup	8 fluid ounces
5⅓ tablespoons	⅓ cup	1 cup	½ pint
8 tablespoons	½ cup	2 cups	1 pint
10⅔ tablespoons	⅔ cup	4 cups	1 quart
12 tablespoons	¾ cup	2 pints	1 quart
16 tablespoons	1 cup	4 quarts	1 gallon

RECIPE LIST